ADOLF HITLER

Jack the Ripper

—HISTORY'S WORST—
ADOLF HITLER

BY JAMES BUCKLEY JR.

Aladdin

New York   London   Toronto   Sydney   New Delhi

ALADDIN

An imprint of Simon & Schuster Children's Publishing Division

1230 Avenue of the Americas, New York, New York 10020

First Aladdin paperback edition August 2017

Text copyright © 2017 by Simon & Schuster, Inc.

Cover illustration copyright © 2017 by Matt Rockefeller

Also available in an Aladdin hardcover edition.

For information about special discounts for bulk purchases, please contact Simon & Schuster Special Sales at 1-866-506-1949 or business@simonandschuster.com.

The Simon & Schuster Speakers Bureau can bring authors to your live event. For more information or to book an event, contact the Simon & Schuster Speakers Bureau at 1-866-248-3049 or visit our website at www.simonspeakers.com.

Cover designed by Laura Lyn DiSiena and Nina Simoneaux

Interior designed by Nina Simoneaux

The text of this book was set in Adobe Caslon Pro.

Manufactured in the United States of America 0717 OFF

2 4 6 8 10 9 7 5 3 1

Library of Congress Cataloging-in-Publication Data

Names: Buckley, James, Jr., 1963– author.

Title: Adolf Hitler / by James Buckley.

Description: First Aladdin hardcover/paperback edition. | New York : Aladdin, 2017. |
Series: History's worst | Audience: Ages 8 to 12. |
Includes bibliographical references and index.

Identifiers: LCCN 2016058534 (print) | LCCN 2016059511 (eBook) |
ISBN 9781481479417 (hardcover) | ISBN 9781481479424 (paperback) |
ISBN 9781481479431 (eBook)

Subjects: LCSH: Hitler, Adolf, 1889–1945—Juvenile literature. | Heads of state—Germany—Biography—Juvenile literature. | Germany—History—1933–1945—Juvenile literature. | World War, 1939–1945—Atrocities—Europe—Juvenile literature.

Classification: LCC DD247.H5 B785 2017 (print) | LCC DD247.H5 (eBook) |
DDC 943.086092 [B]—dc23

LC record available at https://lccn.loc.gov/2016058534

CONTENTS

INTRODUCTION

O n a list of the worst people ever, Adolf Hitler is certainly at or near the top.

He was a racist and a murderer on an epic scale. He led his country into a terrible war, changed the lives of millions and millions of people for the worse, and altered the course of world history, also for the worse. He was selfish, cruel, and heartless.

But as much as we know now about how awful he was, at

the time of his rise to power in the 1930s, millions of Germans loved Hitler and what he had to say. And it wasn't just Germans. Americans, British, and others followed his ideas. Looking back, it's hard to imagine anyone thinking that what he said and what he wanted his people to do were good things. But they did think that. They believed him. They followed him. They did what he and his fellow Nazi leaders told them to do.

Hitler convinced the German people to turn their back on sanity and to seek out and destroy people he said did not belong: Jews, Catholics, Gypsies, homosexuals, developmentally or mentally disabled people, and more. Hitler wanted to create Germany for Germans alone. And he did not believe that all people born in Germany were true Germans. Hitler believed in a special, separate kind of German he called an Aryan: blue-eyed, blond, the "perfect" specimen of humanity. He also wanted to take over more land for the Germans to control, and tried to conquer most of Europe. He sent his armies crashing into neighboring countries, killing and capturing simply because they could. He ignored all the rules and treaties that had held Europe together, and he set himself and his people above others.

He was able to do this in part because people in Germany let him. Of course, millions of Germans were scared to death of him and his Nazis, but amid the fear, millions of others happily followed his every decree and cheered his every word. They supported his efforts to make Germany number one in Europe and his hateful need to kill people he didn't like.

Decades later part of the reason for writing a book about him is to ask, why did people let him do that? Why did they follow him? What made him so attractive? What made Adolf Hitler so popular? And how can we make sure we don't let any more Hitlers enter our world? Those are a lot of big questions. This book will try to give you some of the answers, but will also help you find your own answers to similar questions.

1

CHILDHOOD

The first thing to know about the man who grew up to transform Germany and who wanted Germans to rule the world is that he wasn't German.

Hitler's family was from Austria. In fact, the family name was not even Hitler until 1876. It was originally Schicklgruber. But Hitler's father, Alois, changed that long name to something a little less clunky. Some sources say "Hitler" was a form of another name from Alois's family line.

Alois worked for the Austrian government as a customs inspector, examining people and goods coming across the nation's borders. He had two children—Alois Jr. and Angela—with two different women, and hired his teenage relative Klara to help care for them. Soon Klara was pregnant thanks to Alois. A few years before little Adolf was born, Alois married Klara and they moved into the top floor of an inn in Braunau am Inn, Austria.

The child that caused the marriage, Gustav, was born in 1885 but died shortly after. Another son, Otto, and a daughter, Ida, died very young as well. In the late nineteenth century deadly childhood diseases were not that rare, even in a modern place like Austria.

Alois and Klara kept trying, though, and on April 20, 1889, they welcomed another boy. They named him Adolfus Hitler. And so it started.

WHEN ALOIS GOT a promotion in 1892, the family moved to a new city, Passau. Passau was more than just a new city; it was in a new country. Austria shares a border with Germany, so a few Austrian officials such as Alois lived in that country to help man border stations. Because of this, for the first time in his life, Adolf Hitler was in Germany.

Having lost three other children, Klara was extremely devoted to Adolf. She doted on him constantly, trying to make sure his every need was met, that he was never unhappy. When Adolf was five, his parents added another person to the family, Edmund. Klara still wanted to spoil Adolf, but with a new baby she didn't have a lot of time to spare. Alois was off at work all day while Klara cared for the kids. Adolf took this opportunity to spend more time outside, on the streets of Passau. He got a taste of real freedom for the first time.

But his period of exploration lasted only a short while. In 1895 Alois moved the family to a farmhouse in the smaller, rural town of Hafeld, back in Austria. It was time for Adolf to start school, and after walking an hour to reach the schoolhouse, he did. Of course he also had to walk an hour home. His older half sister, Angela, recalled that even in those early days Adolf was "a little ringleader."[1] The unconditional support of his mother gave Adolf a confidence that he used to try to control every situation. He was very sure of himself from an early age, sure that he knew what was going on and that most other people didn't.

In addition Alois Jr. would say years later that his half brother "was quick to anger from childhood onward and would not listen to anyone. [Klara] always took his side. If he didn't get his way, he got very angry."[2]

Things changed dramatically in 1895. Alois retired from his government job. It altered the family's life completely, as Alois turned out to be terrible at retirement. He spent most of his day at home, and when he was not at home, he was hanging with his friends at bars and pubs. His awful temper was made worse by drink, and he took most of it out on Alois Jr., beating him for any slight. Angela and Edmund didn't fare much better. Adolf was around for these temper tantrums, but most of the anger missed him . . . at first.

The family grew again when a daughter, Paula, was born in 1896. But then the family shrank a year later, when Alois Jr. ran away, unable to put up with his father's beatings. That left Adolf as the oldest male child to face his father's anger. They battled constantly, with Klara often comforting her son after one of the father's rages.

Things improved slightly when Alois moved the family again, this time to Lambach, Austria. Hitler did better in school, with one report card from 1898 showing a stack of ones, the equivalent of As. (In Lambach, as biographer John Toland notes, Hitler went to a nearby church to sing in the choir—apparently the man who would grow to have a powerful speaking voice started out as a lovely young singer—and on his way to the church, he would pass under a stone arch. On it was carved a swastika as part of another design.)

Alois continued to look for a place where he would be comfortable and moved the family again, this time to Leonding, another nearby town but one that was a bit larger and offered him more to do, with concerts, plays, and pubs.

In 1900 the family lost another child when Edmund died of measles. That left Adolf alone with older sister, Angela, and younger sister, Paula. Throughout, Adolf and his father continued to battle. Later his sister Paula would say that Hitler "challenged my father to extreme harshness and . . . got a sound thrashing every day. He was a scrubby little rogue."[3]

At one point when he was eleven, Adolf tried to run away.

The windows of their house were barred for security, and he tried to squeeze through. He couldn't fit. He tried without clothes on and almost made it. Alois discovered him and teased him about having to cover himself with a sheet. If "thrashing" hurt Adolf, this sort of teasing hurt even more.

After every beating and every humiliation, Adolf turned to Klara for comfort. She always supported him, defending him when she could and calming him if possible. Later the family doctor observed that "I have never witnessed closer attachment."[4] Adolf and Klara were making their once-tight relationship even deeper, though as time went on, he became the dominant figure in it.

Hitler was still doing well at school, even as his home life deteriorated. He found that he was also becoming a good artist. He drew pictures of classmates and of the landscape around their town. He was also reading a lot, especially adventure stories. The American writer James Fenimore Cooper wrote tales of the frontier, starring Native Americans, cowboys, trappers, and explorers. Hitler loved these stories and others of a similar nature written by Karl May, a German writer.

Hitler also read about German history, particularly the war that had not long since been concluded with France—the Franco-Prussian War of 1870. (At that time Prussia was a large independent nation; later it would become part of Germany.) In *Mein Kampf (My Struggle)*, the book Hitler wrote in 1924, he described what he felt after reading about the 1870 war. "From then on I became more enthusiastic about everything that was in any way connected with war or . . . soldiering."[5]

In the fall of 1900, Adolf started at a new school that was three miles away in Linz. The school was the equivalent of junior high, but things did not work out well for him at first. He was the new boy, the country boy, and in the beginning he did not fit in. But showing the skills he had used to dominate at his previous school, Hitler worked to become a leader at the new place. He got the other kids to play cowboys and Indians—apparently he had learned to throw a lasso—and talked with them about wars and soldiers.

At the same time, he started reading Germany mythology and saw his first opera by German composer Richard Wagner.

Both of those experiences would become vitally important to him in years to come.

Hitler also continued drawing and painting and was reaching the conclusion that he wanted to be an artist. He did not want to follow in his father's footsteps and enter government service. Not surprisingly, Alois was not happy about this plan. Hitler's boyhood friend August Kubizek later wrote that the choice was "the worst possible insult"[6] to Alois. Hitler himself later wrote that Alois screamed, "An artist! Not as long as I live, never!"[7]

In 1903, Alois Hitler Sr. died.

2

TEENAGE YEARS

With his father gone Hitler was able to try to make his dreams of becoming an artist come true. To move ahead in the Austrian educational system, he had to switch to another school in nearby Steyr. It was too far to travel there every day, so he stayed with another family during the week. It took him away from Klara for the first time in his life. He found that he did not enjoy that situation. His grades dropped, and he paid little attention to school. (One biographer wrote that

Hitler spent more time "shooting rats than studying.")[8]

In 1905, rather than take the final exam that would let him continue his schooling, he dropped out. He convinced Klara to just let him stay at home, painting and basically hanging out. She told the school—and probably thought it was mostly true—that her son was sick and needed rest.

Hitler at this point had few friends, spent most of his time with his mother, and was really, really angry about almost everything. He believed that others were standing in the way of his dream of becoming an artist. His mother let him get his way, but the rest of the world was not quite as cooperative.

Hitler did make one friend during this extended time-out. In August "Gustl" Kubizek, he found a person he could dominate, much as Alois had dominated Adolf and as Adolf was starting to dominate Klara. Through Gustl, Hitler got out in the world a bit more, leaving the house during the day to wander the streets of Linz. They also grew to love opera, attending shows whenever they could. Kubizek, in fact, would go on to a career in music.

In Kubizek, Hitler also found an audience for long speeches about life, politics, art, and more.

"This was not acting, not exaggeration, this was really felt, and I saw he was in dead earnest. I had never imagined that a man could produce such an effect with mere words,"[9] Kubizek said of Hitler, and added that it was Hitler's eyes that were the most mesmerizing, something that many others would feel in the years to come.

Hitler didn't want to take a job of any kind because he felt it was beneath him. From his earliest years, he had an air of superiority. He felt he was better than everyone else. Even though he was rather poor, he tried to dress well, and he carried a cane to look high-class.

Since Hitler had an inability to relate to people other than as the dominant one in the relationship, it was not surprising that he didn't deal well with girls. Biographers have written about his longest "crush," which started in 1904. He saw a girl named Stefanie in the neighborhood and decided that she was for him.

However, as Kubizek relates, Hitler never did anything about it except talk to Kubizek. He got jealous when Stefanie was with other boys, yet he refused to take dancing lessons when Kubizek said she liked to dance. Hitler wrote poems about her that he never showed her. And he shouted at Kubizek when his friend tried to get Hitler to just go and say hello.

IN 1906, HITLER made a trip to Austria's capital, Vienna. Vienna at the time was one of the leading cities of Europe, much larger than the small towns that Hitler had lived in to that point. His visit opened up new vistas. Spending time amid so many people, with so many huge buildings, and with the hustle and bustle of urban life, Hitler found a new way of living.

While on that visit he also saw an opera in a major theater for the first time. In the smaller regional theaters he had visited, the stages were small, the casts less than first-rate. Vienna was one of the world's opera capitals, so Hitler experienced the art at its highest. Many of the shows he saw were based on myths from a long tradition of German storytelling.

WHEN HE GOT back from Vienna, Hitler began to make great plans. He would go to Vienna to study and become a great artist. Kubizek would take music lessons. They would win the lottery, buy an apartment, and build an art studio and a music room.

From his earliest days, whether it was cowboys and Indians, German myths come true, or wild career fantasies, Hitler was a dreamer—with himself and his goals at the center of his fantasies.

He did make one concrete step toward his goal at about this time. He decided to apply for art school in Vienna. Not surprisingly, Klara was thrilled that her boy was trying to make his dreams come true. She was sad to see him want to leave home, but she was probably pleased that he would get out of the house.

As Hitler made his plans, however, the family got more bad news. In January 1907, Klara was diagnosed with breast cancer. At that time there was very little for doctors to do about the disease. They did a surgery called a double mastectomy (removal of both breasts), but they didn't have the follow-up treatments used today to prevent the cancer from spreading or returning. Such a disease was, basically, a death sentence.

The Hitler family moved to a smaller first-floor apartment so Klara could recover from her operation. Hitler stayed with her until he had to return to Vienna in September to take an entrance exam for the art school. For the exam he was asked to submit six sketches, along with having to take written tests. He was stunned when the results came back: "Test drawing unsatisfactory."[10]

For someone who was so confident in all that he did and who had such a massive ego, it was, as he wrote later, "a bolt from the skies"[11] to fail.

The teachers at the art school actually suggested that Hitler try architecture, since his drawings had a precision and form that would suit that career. However, since he had never actually graduated from what was basically high school, and had not taken final exams to get a certificate, Hitler could not go on to a college-level architecture school. Also, he rejected the idea because it did not align with his dream and his opinion of himself as a true artist.

Then he got more bad news. His mother's doctor wrote to him in Vienna in October to say that his mother's condition was worse and she was dying.

For the rest of 1907, Hitler stayed with his mother as she lived her final days. It was a pretty horrible death too, as the surgery wounds never fully healed. Klara was very sick and could not eat or drink much. The medicine used on the wounds was stinging and painful and didn't work well. And Hitler had to watch it happen. He had to watch as his beloved mother, who had supported him through everything, faded away.

When she finally died in late December, Hitler was crushed. The doctor who helped his mother said, "I have never seen anyone so prostrate [overcome] with grief as Adolf Hitler."[12] For his part, Hitler thanked Dr. Bloch, who was Jewish, for all he had done to help his mother. He promised never to forget the doctor or his efforts.

Hitler's father was gone. His mother was gone. His dream of art school was, seemingly, gone. Hitler's life was not turning out as he had hoped.

3

LIFE IN VIENNA

Soon after his mother died, Hitler moved to Vienna, where he hoped to once again see his dream of being an artist come true. For a while he and Kubizek lived together and managed to find enough money to enjoy the city while Hitler supposedly studied and practiced to take the art school exams again.

The two friends went to operas, and Hitler showed his friend around the city that he now called home. Kubizek started taking music classes. But soon he saw that his friend had changed. Kubizek thought that Hitler was angrier than ever, ready to launch into a rant about anything. He got the "impression that Adolf had become unbalanced. He was at odds with the world. Wherever he looked, he saw injustice, hate, and enmity."[13]

Hitler was certainly angry about being rejected from the art school, at one point saying that the whole place should be "blown up."[14] And the pain from his mother's death colored everything in his life.

As his friend studied, Hitler wandered the city during the day, looking at buildings and planning how he would redo the architecture and the streets. He looked for areas where people had too much money, because he wanted to figure out a way to take them out of their palatial places. As he and Kubizek lived in a bug-infested room, seeing so much wealth and beauty was hard on Hitler, who believed he should be a part of that world and not the one he was in.

At night they went to concerts and the opera. Kubizek got free tickets as a music student, or they saved their pfennigs (German coins) for special events. Hitler especially loved when they could see Wagner operas. He saw in Wagner a power and a Germanic beauty that inspired him, and that inspiration grew in years to come.

After finishing his music-school term in June, Kubizek went home in the summer, and Hitler was left alone. Judging by the letters he wrote to his friend, he did very little during that summer, with only an occasional trip to the countryside.

In the fall of 1908, Hitler tried again to enter the art school . . . and once again, he was rejected. This was almost the final straw. Measuring his failure against his friend's success, Hitler basically fell off the map. While Kubizek was still in Linz, Hitler moved out of their apartment in Vienna without telling anyone where he was going. He soon ran out of money and had to live on the streets, sleeping in parks and finding food at churches that ran what were basically soup kitchens. As the weather got worse and winter approached, he survived only by moving into what might today be called a homeless shelter. It was called Asyl fur Obdachlose, a dormitory-style private shelter. The young man who had dreams of becoming a famous, high-class artist, and who railed at injustice—especially against himself—found himself shuffling in line with dozens of others, just hoping for a soft bed. The people living at Asyl still had to go out each day to find food and beg for money, which Hitler did with great shame.

Hitler began working with a man named Hanisch, whom Hitler met at Asyl. Hitler made paintings and drawings, and Hanisch sold them. In this way Hitler began to make a small amount of money. He used it to move to a nicer, larger shelter that had food on the premises. The Männerheim was home to more than five hundred men, in an old but still beautiful building near the Danube River.

As his life slowly improved, Hitler also spent many hours in cafés reading newspapers and talking with fellow artists and jobless men. There was even a lounge at the Männerheim that became a gathering place for men with some education who wanted to talk and debate. Here Hitler once again found the voice he had used with Kubizek to declaim his opinions. Even as he was battling against what he later called one of the worst periods of his life, Hitler was talking, talking, talking. His ability to get angry quickly and then to yell about it for long periods was continuing to be refined. The speaking style that would carry him in the future was slowly being born as he ranted about politics, philosophy, or his lot in life.

Vienna in the years before World War I was a crossroads for various cultures. A lot of Jews had settled there following persecution in Russia. Austrians, Germans, and other Christian Europeans were clearly already angry about this immigration and did not trust the Jews, whom they regarded as non-Christian "others." This situation was made worse by the fact that many Jews became successful bankers, shopkeepers, and merchants while other people in Vienna struggled. (To give an idea of the numbers, in 1860 about 6,000 Jews lived in Vienna. In 1910 about 175,000 Jews lived there.)

During this period in Vienna, Hitler was one of those people who were struggling. Did he too look at the Jews as one of the reasons why he was not doing well? Actually, no, he didn't. The fervent anti-Semitism that marked his years in the future was not evident in those hard years in Vienna. People who knew him then were very surprised about what he said later about the Jews.

What was happening in Vienna that did affect him, however, was what was called the Pan-German Movement. This was a political philosophy that called for the native Germanic people to rise up and remove the outsiders who were slipping into their nation and their culture. That included Jews but also people from the Slavic nations such as Czechs, Slavs, Russians, Poles, and others. The people who followed this movement thought the word "German" referred to a race as much as a nationality.

In fact, Germany had not even been a nation until 1871. Before the nationalist leader Otto von Bismarck united several Germanic states in the 1860s and 1870, "Germans" had instead been Prussians or Bavarians or citizens of more than a dozen other kingdoms, duchies (an area ruled by a duke or duchess), or principalities. Some people outside Germany whose family came from those places looked to this greater Germany as a place to find a new identity. One of those people was Hitler, who had been raised in Austria. People who lived in Austria often identified genetically and culturally with Germany while maintaining a separate political identity as a nation. For his part, Hitler always identified more as a German than as an Austrian.

He was not alone in that feeling, and as the Pan-German Movement grew, it got fiercer in its insistence that everyone had to be put in their place. Non-Germans were not to be included, and anything truly German was to be praised and honored.

In the years to come, the generalized idea of the non-German, and the many groups included in that category, would be replaced almost entirely in Hitler's mind by one group—Jews. But at the start of his growing political thought, it was all about Pan-Germanism, not anti-Semitism.

In 1910, Hitler gained a little financial backing when his aunt Johanna gave him a large sum of money just before she died. Hitler resumed selling paintings, but the inheritance, which he probably hid in his room for safety, let him spend more time talking and reading about politics. The state of Vienna, of Germany, and of Europe were becoming more and more important to him.

Hitler tried one more time to get into the art school but was rejected again. He was successful as a painter, mostly of buildings and street scenes, but the art school was looking for something more "painterly." Hitler's work was very exact and almost photographic. While he dreamed of being an artist, he never really thought like one.

By 1913 his life in Vienna had run its course. The dream of life in Germany remained at the forefront of his mind, as the talk about Pan-Germanism made his next move clear. He had to make his way in the land he saw as central in his world.

For the Austrian Hitler that meant Germany. Over his bed at the Männerheim hung a sign that read WE LOOK FREE AND OPEN, WE LOOK STEADFASTLY, WE LOOK JOYOUSLY ACROSS, TO THE GERMAN FATHERLAND! HEIL![15]

The personal beliefs he was creating, fueled by life in Vienna and by an inner personal drive to find his place, led him to pack up and head for the future.

First stop: Munich.

4

HITLER GOES TO WAR

Munich was the capital of Bavaria, the largest German state. The city of more than six hundred thousand people was what Hitler had been looking for. It was the perfect German city, filled with history, beautiful buildings, and artists, writers, and thinkers. And, most of all, it was overflowing with German patriotism. He would later write that he felt more love "for this city than for any other place I knew, almost from my first hour there. A German city!"[16]

He found a room with a couple named the Popps. As his only trade was drawing, he began to sketch and paint in earnest. The Popps would later write that they saw him leave every day with his art tucked under his arm, ready to find a market and his place in the big city.

He began to spend his days trying to sell his work and his afternoons in the libraries and bookshops. He ate dinner in his room while he read book after book—on philosophy, history, war, and art. Though he was making little money and living hand to mouth, he later called it one of the most special times of his life.

That special time almost ended in February 1914. Though he was living in Germany, he was still an Austrian citizen. So he was expected to do his service in the Austrian army, as all young men were supposed to do at that time. Austrian authorities tracked him down and, with the help of German officials, actually placed him under arrest for evading the army. However, Hitler wrote letters to the Austrian authorities pleading poverty and illness. He was released, though he later had to return to Austria to be examined. Sure enough, months of poor eating meant that

Austrian doctors did reject him for service in their army.

Back in Munich, Hitler's joy continued. He met many German people, debated the world of politics with them, made and sold his art, and studied endlessly. He continued to feel that he was destined to make a difference in the world, even as he remained well down the social ladder.

On June 28, 1914, however, the world changed, not just for Hitler but for everyone in Europe.

That day a Serbian named Gavrilo Princip shot and killed Archduke Ferdinand of Austria. At that time alliances between European nations were very complicated. Within weeks, as a result of the assassination, war was declared among several countries. Germany declared war on Serbia and its ally Russia in order to defend Austria, Germany's ally. England and France soon joined the fighting to defend their Allies, Russia and Serbia.

World War I had begun, and Hitler was overjoyed.

As he later wrote in *Mein Kampf*, "I fell to my knees and thanked Heaven from an overflowing heart for granting me the good fortune of being allowed to live at this time."[17]

Europe in 1914 was a web of connections and treaties. Countries across the region had promised to support one another if any became involved in a conflict. That web needed a single spark to ignite, and it happened on June 28, 1914, when a Serbian teenager assassinated Archduke Franz Ferdinand of the Austro-Hungarian empire.

Mighty Germany was a key ally of Ferdinand's empire, so it declared war on Serbia. Serbia, a smaller nation in the Balkans, was supported by much larger and more powerful Russia. Joining the Russian alliance were France and Great Britain, who were already upset with the German kaiser's plans to expand his nation. The Ottoman Empire joined on the German/Austrian side.

In just weeks the spark of the assassination led to the two sides fighting in the firestorm of World War I. Most historians believe the war was unnecessary and could have been prevented at many points. But once it started, no one would back down, and millions would die.

While Hitler had done all he could to avoid joining the Austrian army, he was eager to join the German military. A nation desperate to fill its ranks of soldiers overlooked his health and took him as a volunteer. He was placed in the Sixteenth Bavarian Regiment, an infantry group. It was known as the List Regiment, after the name of its first commander.

Hitler and the other soldiers were given uniforms, rifles, and packs. After a short period of training near Munich, they piled aboard trains and headed to a camp in Lechfeld, where they would do more drills and learn about the job of being a soldier.

As the train rolled through the countryside, the men sang patriotic songs such as "Watch on the Rhine." Hitler said that at station stops along the way, people gave them food and cheered. His patriotism swelled as they traveled each mile closer to the action. What he had longed for was happening, a chance to fight for his beloved Germany.

For several weeks the men trained at the camp. They marched in the rain and practiced with rifles and bayonets. It was very hard on the men who were used to life in comfortable towns and cities. They slept in tents or outdoors, often in wet conditions. But Hitler was thrilled.

"I'm terribly happy," he wrote to the Popps. "I hope we get to England."[18]

Finally they got their orders and began a four-day march through rain and mud toward the area around Ypres, in Belgium. In the flat fields and meadows around that farming town, fighting was already fierce between German and British soldiers.

In late October, Hitler and the List Regiment finally headed into battle.

"None of us is afraid," Hitler wrote to a friend on the eve of the event. "Everyone is waiting impatiently for the command, 'Forward!'"[19]

5

WORLD WAR I

The reality of war was far different from Hitler's dreams of glory. In that first battle Hitler and his company climbed over trench walls to attack the enemy five times. They fought through rifle and machine-gun fire. Shells exploded over and near them. Soldier after soldier around Hitler fell, but he made it through, even as bullets sliced off his coat sleeve. In fact, later accounts showed that thirty-five hundred men from the List Regiment went into this part of the Ypres battle, but only six hundred remained alive and unhurt. The rest were dead or wounded.

"Like a miracle," Hitler wrote, "I remain safe and alive."[20] Deaths and miracles would continue all around him for the next few years.

Shortly after surviving that first battle, Hitler was transferred out of the front ranks of infantry. His new job was even more dangerous. In a letter to the Popps back in Munich, he wrote, "I have, so to speak, been risking my life every day, looking death straight in the eye."[21] For once Hitler was not exaggerating his role.

He had been made a messenger, or runner, whose job was to take reports and orders back and forth between commanders and various parts of the army. Messengers ran, walked, rode bikes, or hitched rides. They often had to cross enemy territory or dodge bullets and bombs. It was not a safe job, and many runners were killed. Some messages were sent with six separate runners in the hope that one of the messages would make it through. (For many years, Hitler was believed to have regularly been in harm's way. In 2010, new letters from comrades showed that, for the bulk of his time as a runner, he worked well behind the lines in safety. It was to his benefit later in his life to make his work in the war sound much more dangerous. There was some risk, but, it turns out, not nearly as much as he claimed.)

In December, Hitler risked his life to save that of his commander, Lieutenant Colonel Engelhardt. The officer was outside the trenches looking at the enemy position when an attack started. As shells rained down, Hitler and another messenger shielded the colonel with their bodies as they pushed him down into a trench to safety. For his actions Hitler was awarded the Iron Cross (Second Class), one of Germany's highest military honors. He was also promoted to the rank of corporal. He later said it was "the happiest day of my life."[22] A messenger who knew Hitler wrote, "He had found that for which he had been longing for many years, a real home and recognition."[23] (The day after Hitler helped Engelhardt, he left a tent where the colonel and some officers were meeting. Within seconds after Hitler left, a shell struck the tent and several men were killed. Hitler escaped injury.)

The young artist who had felt destined for greatness and who had passionately spoken about how he thought the world should be was now a war hero. The status gave him even more inner strength. He believed that the honor cemented his special place. And by continuing to survive the war, even as tens of thousands of others around him died or were maimed, his sense of special status grew. At one point he told his fellow soldiers, "Just wait until my time comes. You will hear much more about me later."[24]

Also growing was his hatred of the English, Germany's main opponent even though the battlegrounds were in Belgium and France. The "Tommies," as the English soldiers were known, were considered evil by the Germans, especially Hitler. He began to hate them for challenging the great German people, let alone for what they were doing to his fellow soldiers.

During Christmas in 1914 an odd truce began between the enemy lines. Soldiers on both sides sang carols, shared cigarettes, and put off killing one another in the spirit of the holiday. Though the killing began again soon after, Hitler was reportedly disgusted with the idea of such a Christmas truce. One fellow soldier said Hitler was "an embittered opponent of the fraternization"[25] (which means "fellowship").

Because of his devotion to duty and his zeal for action, Hitler was respected by most of his fellow soldiers. They also liked the little drawings he did for them. (As with his reputation as a messenger, Hitler's story took some hits with new evidence from fellow soldiers. Letters were found that contradicted this rosy picture of Corporal Hitler as being less well-liked than the popular myth had it.) He made small portraits of them or drew scenes from the barracks or trenches that soldiers could mail home to their families. But though they thought he did his messenger job well, Hitler did not make many friends among his fellow soldiers, even the other runners. In fact, it was said that he never got mail from home either, including Christmas presents. He remained the strongest patriot among them, sure of their cause even as the mud, rain, and freezing temperatures—to say nothing of the terrible food and the horrible fighting—dragged down morale. When some soldiers began to question the strategy of trench warfare or the decisions of the commanders, Hitler yelled at them. He defended the idea of the war along with how it was being fought. He believed that Germany would win, no matter what.

A letter he wrote in February 1915 showed that his long-studied thoughts about what Germany should be were starting to come together more firmly as he experienced a war to defend the nation. "Those of us who are lucky enough to return to the Fatherland will find it a purer place, less riddled with foreign influences,"[26] he wrote in a letter to an acquaintance from Munich.

By "foreign influences" he mostly meant Russians who were trying to spread Marxism in Germany and other places, but his view of outsiders began to more clearly include Jewish people, even German-born Jews. Some German Jews were involved in a growing interest in Marxism, the philosophy that would soon create the Soviet Union in Russia. Hitler hated the ideas of Marxists and in his mind merged all Jews with that philosophy. The fire that would create the Holocaust was starting to smolder.

Not long after the new year, Hitler did make one friend, a fox terrier he called Foxl. The little dog would remain with him for most of the rest of the war.

There was one interesting footnote from Hitler's early days as a soldier. World War I was the first to include poison gas as a weapon. Both sides used it. Soldiers were issued gas masks that they were supposed to put on quickly as soon as gas was identified. Hitler at the time had a wide, thick mustache, very much like German generals and officials. The gas mask would not fit tightly over the thick hairs, and gas could leak in. According to a report found in 2006 from a fellow soldier, Hitler was ordered to shave his mustache so the mask would fit. Instead he trimmed it to leave only the center couple of inches. The "toothbrush" style mustache would remain on his face for the rest of his life and give him an unmistakable visual identity.

The war would leave many other marks on Hitler as well.

6

A SOLDIER

Christmas in 1915 did not see a truce, as had happened in 1914, but it did see horrible rain that kept the trenches flooded. His fellow soldiers opened packages from home, but Hitler got none. One account said that he did not say a word for more than three days during the holiday. His comrades felt that he was setting himself apart. In his mind, he was remaining above them all, focusing on bigger things than presents.

Throughout the spring Hitler continued his job delivering messages. The fighting was less frequent, however, as the weather prevented both sides from doing very much. In June, as the weather cleared, Hitler's regiment took part in one of the deadliest battles of the war. Known as the Battle of the Somme, for the river in France near where it happened, it cost tens of thousands of lives on both sides.

The war was not fought on wide-open fields or across valleys. Instead each side had dug miles of trenches, complete with bunkers, offices, and sleeping areas. They moved within their own trenches, lobbing shells at each other. At some point they each went over the top of the trenches, charging headlong toward the other in an attempt to reach the enemy. In nearly all cases such attacks were beaten back with merciless gunfire. One side fired from a protected trench while the other ran toward the oncoming bullets. It was slaughter.

THE TRENCHES

Technology played a deadly role in World War I. New weapons changed how war was fought. Up to this point, most wars had been fought by large groups of men marching toward each other, firing single-shot rifles. But in the early 1900s deadly new weapons changed the rules. Machine guns spewed out hundreds of bullets in seconds. Artillery shells became bursting scraps of metal instead of single cannonballs. A new material called barbed wire was strung for miles and slowed marches to a crawl. Poison gas was used for the first time.

To deal with these weapons, the Allies and then the Germans dug long trenches in the open plains of France, Belgium, and the Netherlands. There they could hide from the shells and machine guns in some safety. They could retreat from gas attacks to put on masks.

The bad part was that in order to advance on the enemy, they had to leave the trenches. These tragic attacks, called "going over the top" of the trenches, resulted in huge numbers of deaths and injuries. And in the end neither side could really advance. Trench warfare was muddy, deadly, awful, and ineffective, but it defined how most of the war was fought.

At one point in the battle, Hitler was sent out into that hellish place to deliver a key message. He somehow made it and also dragged back another runner who had been injured.

The awful struggle of the Somme went on for more than three months. Neither side could advance past the other. The Allied side—British and French troops—had more than six hundred thousand men killed or wounded. On the German side more than four hundred thousand were casualties.

In October one of the casualties was Hitler. As he awaited orders, his trench was hit by a shell. When such shells exploded, they split up into hundreds of small pieces of hot, fast-moving metal. The metal sprayed in a deadly circle from the shell. In this blast one of the pieces struck Hitler in the thigh, opening a large wound. Though he pleaded to stay, he was sent to a hospital to recover. After he could walk again, he spent part of his recovery in Berlin, which was his first visit to Germany's largest and most important city. What he found there angered him. There was not enough support for the troops doing the fighting, he felt. He did not feel honored by the people he met. He was aghast at how much influence Marxists, known as "Reds," had in the city. He was also shocked, he wrote later, at how many Jews were safely back home while Germans fought at the front. (In fact, Hitler was wrong; more than twelve thousand German Jews died fighting for the kaiser, among many, many more who also served in the armed forces.)

By January, Hitler was again asking to return to the regiment, and in March he made it back. Foxl was overjoyed to see him, apparently. For his part Hitler was thrilled to be back among the soldiers. He felt much more at home there, where the reason for fighting was clear and the job he was doing felt important.

That work began in earnest when the regiment was sent once again to fight near Ypres. For more than two weeks the troops huddled in trenches as artillery shells rained down, as planes dropped other bombs, and even as gas attacks poured over them. Again, however, the trench warfare did nothing more than kill soldiers. Men were stabbed, shot, gassed, blown up, or even drowned in water-filled trenches. It was later calculated that there was a dead body on just about every square yard of the battlefield. The worst fighting happened near a place called Passchendaele, and an infamous battle is known by this name. No real territory or victory was gained, but as many as seven hundred thousand men are believed to have lost their lives on this killing field.

Sadly for Hitler, during his move back from the front lines, Foxl disappeared. The dog might have been taken by another soldier going forward, but Hitler never knew for sure.

In the fall of 1917, Hitler took his first official time off from the fighting. He visited the beautiful city of Dresden. He returned to Berlin and had a much better time, visiting museums and beginning to like the city more and more.

Life at the front in the winter, however, was very bad. Low food supplies meant that the men had to scrounge for food, eating rats, cats, and dogs when necessary. Hitler, according to fellow soldiers, refused to eat dog, in honor of Foxl. Life back home in Germany was also very hard, with people starving or being forced to eat sawdust with their potatoes. By January 1918 the people had had enough. Hundreds of thousands of workers went on strike, refusing to do their jobs unless the imperial government provided them with more food.

Hitler saw this as a betrayal of the soldiers. "What was the army fighting for if the homeland itself no longer wanted victory? The soldier is expected to fight, and the homeland goes on strike?"[27] He blamed Marxists for the strikes, and by extension, the Jews.

Back on the battlefield in the summer, Hitler continued to excel as a soldier. His regiment took part in battle after battle. In June he was coming back from delivering a message when he came across several French soldiers. Drawing his pistol, he took them prisoner. His commanders continued to notice his daring and spirit. "There was no situation that would have prevented him from volunteering for the most difficult . . . and dangerous tasks,"[28] wrote one colonel.

Another officer saw what Hitler had done and awarded the young corporal the Iron Cross, First Class. It was the highest honor Germany gave a soldier, and the commander who arranged it was named Hugo Gutmann. He was one of the tens of thousands of German Jews who fought in the army for the kaiser.

That army, however, was on the way to overall defeat. By the end of the summer of 1918, it was clear to the kaiser that his forces could not win. The soldiers felt beaten. The people back home were rising up in anger. It was frustrating for Hitler to face this. At one point he got into a terrible fistfight with another soldier who had said it was "stupid" to keep fighting the war. But the fighting did go on. In September, Hitler's regiment was sent once again to Ypres.

On October 14, during the long weeks of fighting, a gas attack rolled over the trenches where Hitler and his comrades waited. Even though his mustache was neatly trimmed, his mask did not keep the gas out. Hitler was overcome by the poison fumes. He was blinded by the gas. The loss of vision would probably be temporary, doctors told him, but he could not be sure.

Hitler was sent to a hospital to recover. For weeks he lay in his bed, unable to see, angry that he could not be with his fellow soldiers in the fight. On November 12 he got even worse news. The chaplain at the hospital told Hitler and the other soldiers that Germany had surrendered. The war was over. Germany had lost.

Hitler was furious. Blind and unable to get out of bed, he raged not only against the enemies who had won on the battlefield, but also against the politicians he blamed for giving up. He believed that the Social Democratic Party, which was growing in power in Germany, had given up too easily. Of course, it was the kaiser's government, not the political party, that had lost the war. Hitler, however, believed that the Reds and the Jews had let down the army. He felt personally betrayed.

"I threw myself on the bed and buried my head in my pillow," he later wrote. "I had not cried since the day I stood at my mother's grave. Now I couldn't do anything else."[29]

Hitler the proud patriot had marched into war in 1914, eager to see his beloved country take its place as the ruler of Europe. A blind, bitter, wounded, angry Hitler lay in a bed in 1918 as his world collapsed around him.

7

AFTER THE WAR

World War I had officially ended on November 11, 1918, in a ceremony conducted at the eleventh hour of the eleventh day of the eleventh month. While November 11 marked the end of fighting, the war's conclusion was the final catalyst for Hitler's rise to world prominence.

The first steps in Hitler's rise came in the weeks leading up to the end of the war, as Hitler lay blind and powerless in a hospital. The German people had had enough of the kaiser and his government and his war. In city after city they began to revolt, sometimes led by leftist leaders. Workers left their posts, people marched in the streets, and battles raged as Germans fought against Germans.

President Woodrow Wilson of the United States said he would sign a war-ending agreement only with a democratic government. Seeing the writing on the wall, Kaiser Wilhelm II stepped down on November 9, ending the German empire. A man named Friedrich Ebert was named chancellor, or president, of a new German republic. However, not everyone was happy about this development.

In Berlin a group calling itself the Spartacists wanted a strong, central leadership. They formed a tough-guy group called the Free Corps that took it on themselves to enforce order as they saw it. They actually prevented a Communist takeover of Berlin in the weeks following the war.

THE RISE OF COMMUNISM

While Germany was battling in World War I, one of their opponents was undergoing a vast change of its own. In Russia the imperial rulers were being overthrown by a civil war. With the czar gone, the fight was about how Russia would be ruled. By 1921 the Communists had won that battle of "Red" vs. "White" Russians.

Communism is a political idea in which the state owns all the goods and companies, while the people are all supposed to share equally in success . . . or failure. It was first proposed by the German writer Karl Marx in the 1870s. By 1917 the Russian Communist (or "Bolshevik") leader was Vladimir Ulyanov, known as Lenin. He led a revolution that turned Russia into the world's first and largest Communist state. It was called the Union of Soviet Socialist Republics (USSR).

Inspired by Lenin and the Soviets, people in other countries, including Germany, tried to create similar Communist revolutions. They didn't succeed, but people across Europe, and even some in America, saw the ideal of Communism as a secure way forward for the world. Unfortunately, Lenin's successors changed those ideals into something more like a dictatorship. Unfortunately, Lenin's successors changed those ideals into something more like a dictatorship, which lasted in what became the Soviet Union until 1991.

Finally, a national election put an official German government in place. None of the competing groups—right, left, and center—got enough seats in the new National Constituent Assembly to govern effectively. The fighting and arguing among Germans continued.

Into this mix of confusion and distrust stepped Adolf Hitler, released from the hospital after the temporary blindness caused by the gas had worn off and still very angry. He was still in the army, however, as he needed to work. In early 1919 he was sent to help a group within the army that was watching the revolutionaries and German Communists as they plotted against the newly elected government. Some Germans had been inspired by Russia and wanted to bring the new Communist ideas to the new Germany. Given his intense love of Germany and his ability to speak in public, Hitler at first went to talk to soldiers and make sure they didn't go over to the Communists.

He had an even harder job of that after the Treaty of Versailles was signed on June 28, 1919. This was the document that laid out the terms of Germany's official defeat in World War I, and the terms were not at all good for Germany. The nation was forced to take official blame for the whole conflict. They were also told to pay enormous sums—what would today be billions and billions of dollars—to the Allied nations as reparations for all that Germany had done. Other terms of the treaty took land back from the German Republic and also strictly limited the Germans' ability to have military forces of any size.

For Hitler the treaty was pretty much the last straw. He saw it as a complete surrender to the enemies and as a stab in the back to the German people. Even as he seethed, however, he had to work.

In the fall of 1919 he was assigned by the army to infiltrate the small German Workers' Party. The government was taking a close look at all the many radical groups working against them. Hitler was, in effect, a spy.

Amazingly, instead of reporting on the group, he ended up joining them. He would not make this clear to his superiors for some time but instead reported tidbits of the meetings back to them in order to be able to continue attending.

He met with the group's leaders after going to some general meetings. What they were saying matched perfectly with what he was thinking. Germany had been sold down the river, Jews and Reds were the main cause, Germany must rise again to its rightful place.

Slowly he grew in importance in the group, giving a few speeches that were very well received. His intense style was very different from the careful and thoughtful manner of other speakers. He didn't talk; he yelled. He didn't persuade; he ranted.

About this time he met more people who fueled his hatred of the Jews. The writer Dietrich Eckart was particularly influential. Eckart was a strong believer in racist views of humanity. Plus, Hitler saw Jews leading several groups that took over German cities, such as Kurt Eisner in Munich and Rosa Luxemburg in Berlin, along with Jews in prominent roles in Communist uprisings in other countries.

Finally, Hitler was asked to join the executive committee of the Workers' Party. This was a big step. He had wanted to someday start his own party, but now here was a chance to re-create one already in place. Still, he considered it for a while. Then, he wrote later, "I finally came to the conviction that I had to take this step . . . It was the most decisive resolve of my life. From here there was and could be no turning back."[30]

In September 1919, Hitler for the first time put his horrible thoughts about Jews on paper, in a letter he wrote to a Workers' Party supporter.

About the Jews, he wrote, "[The Jew] burrows into the democracies sucking the good will [sic] of the masses, crawls before the majesty of the people but knows only the majesty of money. His activities result in racial tuberculosis of the people."[31]

The smoldering embers of his hatred that had been burning for years were now a huge flame, and soon he would have a way to use it to spread the fire.

THROUGHOUT THE LATTER part of 1919, Hitler was still actually working for the army. In fact, he got permission from his officers to take further steps with the Workers' Party, helping it organize its offices and recruit new members. The army continued to think that helping this Workers' Party stay on the positive side of the government would be a good thing.

On October 16, Hitler gave a speech to the largest Workers' Party gathering to date. He "electrified" the crowd, according to witnesses.[32] He was coming into his own as a speaker, as a leader, and as a believer.

"I spoke for thirty minutes, and what before I had simply felt within me, without in any way knowing it, was now proved by reality: I could speak!" he wrote later in *Mein Kampf*.[33]

Emboldened, Hitler worked with others in the Workers' Party to draft a set of organizing ideas, a sort of statement of principles. They came up with twenty-five points.

On February 24, 1920, Hitler spoke to a gathering of more than two thousand people. Some disagreed with the first part of his speech. In a move that would become standard, anyone who disagreed was beaten, punched, or harassed, or simply kicked out of the room. He spoke for more than two hours, piling up his points one by one, until all twenty-five of the statements in the party had been "voted" on by the shouting mob of people. Reject the Versailles Treaty! All Germans unite in one nation! Share riches with everyone, not just the top! And, most ominously, no Jews in public office, kick out Jews who came after the start of the war, treat all Jews as aliens, and more.

For the small party it was a huge day. For Hitler it was a triumph and the proof he needed that everything he had long hoped for would happen. He saw that he could be a true leader of a movement. "When I closed the meeting, I was not alone in thinking that now a wolf had been born, destined to burst in upon the herd of seducers of the people."[34]

Hitler, of course, was the wolf.

On March 31, 1920, the wolf finally left the army pack. Corporal Hitler was no more. Citizen Hitler took his place.

As summer wore on, Hitler continued to give speeches to rally people to his cause. He also chose the party's new symbol: a black swastika in a white circle on a red flag. That year, under Hitler's urging, the fast-growing German Workers' Party changed its name to the National Socialist German Workers' Party. In German the new name was written as Nationalsozialistische Deutsche Arbeiterpartei.

Soon everyone called the party by a nickname.

The Nazis.

8

LEADER OF THE NAZIS

While Hitler was making his moves in Munich, the rest of Germany continued to be in turmoil as well. Communist groups were still gathering strength and in fact had taken control of some major cities. The official German government, which set up in a town called Weimar, as Berlin was not deemed safe enough, continued to use the still mostly unofficial Free Corps to keep order. The army had been shrunk dramatically due to the Treaty of Versailles. The Free Corps, filled with angry former army members and with people who were looking for a way to take that anger out, viscously fought against Communists, without mercy or any attention to laws.

In April 1920, Free Corps members crushed a Red rebellion in a part of Germany called the Ruhr. One member of the corps wrote gleefully to a friend about shooting "10 Red Cross nurses on sight."[35]

While Germany fell apart, Hitler's hatred of Jews was growing by leaps and bounds. He got more fuel for his fire in the summer of 1920, when a document called *The Protocols of the Elders of Zion* was published for the first time in Germany. The document, first written in the late 1890s, was claimed to be the secret document laying out the Jewish plan for world domination. It was entirely false, but it was quickly used by Dietrich Eckart and others to continue to blame the Jews for everything. Sadly, it's still quoted by racists even though it is completely made up.

For Hitler this was a signal to ramp up attacks. In August he gave a two-hour speech called "Why We Are Against the Jews." He took it all the way back to the Bible, where some sections seem to say that Jews killed Christ, and brought his rants all the way through the war and to *The Protocols of the Elders of Zion*. His speech was a collection of lies, but it was greeted with applause and ovations.

In early 1921, Hitler added another way to spread his message of hate. He convinced the Nazi Party to buy a major Munich newspaper called the *Münchner Beobachter*. Eckart and others raised the money needed, and the Nazis soon were filling the paper with article after article against the Jews, against Communists, and *for* the Nazis.

In the summer of 1921, when Hitler was in Berlin meeting with other opposition leaders from other parties opposed to the ruling Social Democrats, some members of the Nazi Party decided that he was going too far. They were pleased with the growing membership but objected to the intense and violent approach Hitler was taking. They voted to remove him from his leadership post within the propaganda part of their party.

Hitler was not amused. He simply resigned from the party and waited for people to change their minds. As news of the proposed change spread, many party members called for Hitler's return. These members didn't agree with the few moderate people in leadership positions. They wanted their man. He said he would come back, but only if he was made party chairman. "I make these demands, not because I am power hungry, but because recent events have more than convinced me that without an iron leadership the party will . . . cease to be what it was supposed to be," he said.[36] Soon the full party got the chance to vote him into the top spot.

On July 29, 1921, the results were announced. The vote was 543 to 1. Adolf Hitler was now officially the führer (FYURE-er), or leader, of the Nazi Party. It was a role he would not give up until the day he died.

It's worth asking here, why were people so enamored of Hitler? Looking back on what people said about him, and watching them in newsreels from later on, it's hard to understand, unless you were actually there, in the shoes of Germans, in the spirit of their times, seeing and hearing him in person. People said he was mesmerizing, that he was almost hypnotic in his speeches. They raved about his intensity, how foam flecked his lips and his voice became almost a screech as he went on and on. Non-German observers even noted the inner fanaticism that came out when Hitler spoke. One historian wrote that he witnessed "hypnotic mass-excitement."[37] Perhaps it was one of those "you had to be there" experiences, but for those who were there, Hitler's speeches were something they never forgot.

Meanwhile, speeches were not the only way the Nazis were getting their point across. Remember how people who disagreed were beaten up at early Hitler speeches? As he gathered more power, the beatings got worse . . . and more organized. Led by a former army captain named Ernst Röhm, and inspired by the success of the Free Corps, the Nazis formed the Sturmabteilung (which means "storm detachment"), or SA. Dressed in a uniform that earned the members the nickname "Brownshirts," the SA were the street-level enforcers of the ideals of the party. They attacked Jews, they tore down flags and posters of rival parties, and they interrupted meetings and speeches of groups they disagreed with. On one occasion, with Hitler at their head, they broke up a meeting at a bar, an event which turned into a glass-throwing brawl, with Hitler on a table shouting encouragement. They were, basically, thugs.

Hitler didn't care. In fact, he encouraged it. "Cruelty impresses," he said. "People need a good scare. They want somebody to make them afraid."[38]

Later he was quoted as saying, "Our motto shall be, if you will not be a German, I will bash your skull in. We are convinced that we cannot succeed without a struggle."[39]

Throughout 1922 the Nazis continued to attract followers in Munich, and soon in other cities in Bavaria. Hitler spoke to larger and larger crowds, feeding them his brand of anti-Semitic hatred, but also feeding their need to hear a leader call for a return to a united, powerful, all-German Germany. Nazi Party membership grew to more than fifty thousand people.

Meanwhile, in Italy a man named Benito Mussolini was doing very much the same thing as Hitler, but on a grander scale. He used the same sort of fiery, nationalistic speeches, as well as street thugs ("Blackshirts," in his case) to scare and threaten people. In late 1922 Mussolini succeeded in taking his movement nationwide and gained control of Italy.

After that, being the führer of a small party in Munich was not enough for Hitler. He saw his destiny on a larger stage. The corporal from the trenches was ready to take over the whole country.

9

JAIL

In early 1923, French officials, tired of waiting for the German government to start making its war payments, decided to take something else instead. They marched in and took over the Ruhr valley area of Germany. As a result the German government decided, after long thought (and after the threat of losing more territory), to start paying back some of the reparations demanded by the Treaty of Versailles. Because the government was going to have to pay huge sums to the winners of the war, the value of German money took a huge hit. In Germany everyone was suddenly scrambling for cash, which was worth less and less every day.

For Hitler and the Nazis this was the last straw. They could not accept that their government would give up not only land but also desperately needed money. Hitler called for a bold move, and he thought he had the muscle to back it up.

His plan was to kidnap leaders of the Munich government and force them to turn power and Bavaria over to him. Though Bavaria was part of Germany, it maintained many of its own governmental systems, much like a US state. On November 8 the Nazis learned that a state government meeting was being held at a beer hall in Munich.

More than six hundred SA members stormed the building, led by Hitler waving a pistol. They poured into the meeting, knocking aside anyone who opposed them. Hitler himself took the stage and corralled three of the key government leaders in a room. He forced them to turn over control to him. Hitler returned to the stage to proclaim victory. Amid the pandemonium, he declared, "I am going to fulfill the vow I made to myself five years ago when I was a blind cripple in the military hospital—to know neither rest nor peace until the November criminals had been overthrown, until on the ruins of the wretched Germany of today there should have arisen once more a Germany of power and greatness, of freedom and splendor."[40]

As Hitler spoke, however, the Munich leaders simply left the building and escaped. The police soon came and broke up the meeting.

The next day Hitler and two thousand SA troops, also known as storm troopers, marched in to take the city they thought they had won. But the leaders who had "given up" to Hitler the night before had been just playing along with him. They reported the attempted takeover, and the army was ready for Hitler, Röhm, the government's SA forces, and the Nazi party's own security men. A battle commenced. Sixteen Nazis were killed by the police and army forces, and hundreds were arrested. Hitler himself suffered a dislocated shoulder in the melee. He had been linking arms with a comrade, who had been shot, and when the man fell, he yanked Hitler's shoulder out of joint. Hitler's personal bodyguard, Ulrich Graf, then leaped in front of Hitler and was shot several times. The bullets would have struck Hitler. As Graf fell, he landed on Hitler.

Hitler escaped and hid out with a sympathetic friend. He was in terrible pain from his injured shoulder. The next morning, in fact, one of the women he was staying with had to convince him not to shoot himself. "How can you leave all the people you have gotten interested in your idea of saving your country—and then take your own life?"[41] She took the gun away from him and hid it.

Hitler was arrested the next day and charged with treason for leading what became known as the Beer Hall Putsch, the latter word being a German term for a takeover. The attempted putsch was a failure for Hitler, but as he had before, he turned it into a triumph.

After gaining public notice for going on a two-week hunger strike, Hitler was put on trial. For more than three weeks he got a chance to speak to the court and to public listeners. As usual, he enthralled just about everyone with his familiar themes of German nationalism, anti-Semitic hatred, and revolt against the government that he still accused of stabbing Germany in the back in 1918.

"I alone bear the responsibility [for the attempted putsch]," he said at one point. "But I am not a criminal because of that. If today I stand here as a revolutionary, it is as a revolutionary against the revolution. There is no such thing as high treason against the traitors of 1918."[42]

In the end he was convicted, but he was sentenced to only five years, with the promise of getting out well before then.

He was even given a very comfortable space in jail, with several rooms, and also a typewriter. With the help of a visiting Nazi official named Rudolf Hess, who took down his every word, Hitler spent most of his short, nine-month jail stint writing a book. When he was released in December 1924, his world and political philosophy was ready to be shared in print. The book was released in the summer of 1925 and was called *Mein Kampf*. It covered in great detail his life to that point, his views on Germany, his views on how he had all the answers, and, most clearly, how he believed the Jews were at the heart of all that was wrong with the world. He detailed his opinions on just about every race, ranking them from top to bottom. At the top, he declared, were Aryans, the blue-eyed, blond men of German background. They were at the top of the ladder, he said, the master race. Of course, he said that Jews and others were at the bottom of the ladder and should serve and live at the Aryans' pleasure. Also, since Aryans were the master race, they needed the most space, so Germany should be able to take whatever land it wanted.

Mein Kampf pretty much laid out all the things that happened in the coming years, from the destruction of Jews to the expansion of Germany, from attitudes of a master race to a movement dominated by one man. It was like a to-do list for taking and holding power but with an awful, racist twist. In one section he suggested that if only Jews had been "forced to submit to poison gas,"[43] the recent war would have been won by Germany. It was a horrible foreshadowing of the destruction to come.

The book sold very well when it came out, and Hitler, for the first time in his life, was soon financially secure. The royalties from the book would make him a rich man over time.

When Hitler was released from jail, he told his followers that he and the Nazis would have to begin again. It would take him many years to have another shot at ultimate power.

10

THE RISE TO POWER

Those years after Hitler's stint in jail included a series of events that led directly to Hitler's taking over Germany. Some of the actions were started by groups directed by him. Some came from outside Germany, as world events or movements affected a nation still recovering from war. Most of the actions, however, were born in the fevered mind of a man convinced that he and he alone could and should rule Germany, and remake the country in the way that matched his increasingly awful worldview.

Soon after Hitler's release from prison, his public speeches were outlawed by the government of Bavaria, which he had, after all, tried to take over in the putsch. He managed to speak loudly and often, however, to many gatherings in that German state and elsewhere. The Nazi Party remained in action and he remained as its leader.

Hitler, of course, was convinced of the rightness of his cause. He still had tens of thousands of supporters in Bavaria and around the nation. Under Röhm, the SA continued to grow, though the government officially had banned them from operating in the open and from wearing the brown shirts that were their uniform. Hitler also built parts of the party that would remain throughout the coming war, including the Hitler Youth. (At first only party members' children joined, but by the late 1930s, nearly every German child would be forced to take part in the group's activities. Not surprisingly, those activities were essentially designed to brainwash children into fully believing in Hitler as a leader and the Nazis as the source of all belief.)

During this period Hitler also began to have a little bit of a life outside the party. He became involved with his niece, Geli Raubal. Hitler's half sister, Angela, was Geli's mother, so it was more than a little creepy, but the pair seemed to get along famously, going on picnics and to the theater. Were they lovers? Most biographers think they were, but Hitler never really said. They lived in an apartment in Munich by the middle of 1929. But later that year Hitler met Eva Braun, who worked for a Nazi Party photographer. She would soon take Geli's place.

In elections in the later 1920s, after Hitler's time in jail, the Nazis slowly added seats in the Reichstag, the name for the German Republic's legislature. In the fall of 1929 the party held a massive rally at Nuremberg. Hitler and the Nazis had become a growing strength in the German government, but, frankly, things were improving in the country. The 1920s had seen a steady rise in income and employment. People were starting to forget the horrors and hardships of the war. With things going well for most people, it was harder for Hitler to convince them that they should be afraid of Jews, Communists, and any other supposed enemies.

But events around the world turned Germany's mood in Hitler's favor. On October 24, 1929, the United States stock market crashed. Almost overnight, billions of dollars of value disappeared. Businesses closed, banks closed, people lost their life savings. One of the results was that US banks and businesses, desperate for cash, told German banks and businesses that they had to repay loans made in the years after the war. That was not possible, and the Great Depression spread quickly to Germany, and to other European nations.

Hitler realized this was a key opening for him. His message of German nationalism and of fear of the outsider now had an audience desperate for answers. The nation was losing money and jobs. Hitler claimed that the reason was not economics but the Jewish conspiracy and other outside forces. In 1930 an election made the Nazis the second-largest party in the Reichstag, behind the Center Party, which had taken over after the Social Democrats.

In 1931 Hitler's private life collided with his public one for one of the few times in his life. He had been spending more time with Eva Braun, and Geli was jealous. In September of that year,

Geli was found dead of a gunshot in their Munich home. The gun lay by her side, and it looked like suicide. To this day there is no clear answer as to whether Hitler had her killed so he could be with Braun or whether the young woman could not handle the stress of a relationship with her uncle, who was quickly becoming a national figure. In any case, soon after Geli's death Braun and Hitler more officially became a couple. In keeping with his devotion to the Nazi cause, however, Hitler never appeared in public with Braun. Many Germans learned about her only after the couple's death in 1945.

Meanwhile, politics went on. In 1932 a presidential election was held. Hitler put his name on a national ballot for the first time. (Interestingly, Hitler was not a German citizen when he made the decision to run. He had never done the work to become one, remaining officially an Austrian. To run for president he had to get his citizenship papers quickly, which he did with help from Nazi Party officials.) Hitler got only 30 percent of the vote (there were several men running), while the winner again was General Paul von Hindenburg, by then eighty-six years old, who had been president since 1925.

The SA, which had been outlawed by Bavaria after the putsch, had been waiting to act. It finally could after the Nazis pushed through legislation that changed the rules banning the SA. Freed again, the Brownshirts hit the streets and caused havoc, assaulting Jews and Communists and creating an atmosphere of fear in several large cities.

Seeing Hitler's and the Nazis' growing strength, the Hindenburg government desperately looked for a way to get him under control. Amazingly, in 1933 Hindenburg appointed Hitler to the key post of chancellor, a sort of second-in-command. The president had been pressured by businessmen and politicians. The rising power of the Nazi Party meant that Hindenburg had to do something to appease them. Hindenburg's decision can now be seen as a huge error, but at the time, he thought that by letting Hitler in, the chancellor could be controlled by the remaining Center Party leaders, Social Democrats, and other officials. Hindenburg thought that he could keep Hitler's ideas from spreading. He could not have been more wrong.

Within hours the Brownshirts were marching in the streets, carrying torches and singing. Their leader was now, basically, *the* leader. While Berliners watched the takeover of their neighbor-hoods, people around Germany listened on the radio to excited commentators describing the scene. One biographer recounted a woman remembering "the crashing tread of the feet, the pomp of the red and black flags, the songs that were . . . both aggres-sive and sentimental."[44] Meanwhile, the French ambassador to Germany wrote about a "river of fire"[45] that he saw from his embassy as torch-lit parades filled the streets. And one for-mer German general sent a prediction to Hindenburg. Erich Ludendorff sent a telegram that read in part, "I prophesy to you this evil man will plunge our Reich into the abyss and will inflict immeasurable woe on our nation. . . ."[46]

THE GENERAL

With a thick handlebar mustache, Paul von Hindenburg looked every bit the classic Prussian general. He started with military school at age eleven and never stopped. He fought in the 1870 Franco-Prussian War and later was the field mar-shal (top military leader) for German forces in World War I. In 1925 he was elected as the nation's second president when a republic was formed in the years after the war.

Popular among the people for his war service, he held the office of president during rough times in the late 1920s and early 1930s. As Hitler and the Nazis rose, however, Hindenburg was growing old and weakening. His appointment of Hitler as chancellor opened the door to Nazi power. The old general died in 1934.

As chancellor in early 1933, Hitler called for yet more elections. In Germany's system at the time, elections were not held on a regular annual or biannual schedule, but rather they were called when the government decided. Sometimes, as in this case, several times a year. As the voting neared for this election, Hitler went on the radio and traveled. He spoke more calmly, promising that things would get better. This time, however, he didn't talk much about the Jews or other outsiders. He was almost normal. He sounded, for once, not that threatening. People outside the Nazi Party began to think, *Maybe this guy's all right.*

When the results of the new elections in early spring

came back, Hitler finally got what he wanted—control of the Reichstag.

Along with his phony attitude in the campaign, he was helped by a disaster that was probably caused by the Nazis in their zeal to show Germans that there was much to fear. On February 27, 1933, the enormous building that was home to the Reichstag in Berlin was destroyed by fire. The massive domed building was a symbol of the German democratic government. Hitler and the Nazis claimed that Communist forces had done the dirty work. In fact, it was a former Communist named Marinus van der Lubbe who had set the fire, intending to spur Germans to revolution. That news was not public for a while, however, and Hitler was the first to blame the event on a wider Communist conspiracy instead of a lone arsonist.

"This is a God-given signal," Hitler said. "We must crush this murderous pest with an iron fist."[47]

Led by the Nazis in the Reichstag and forced by Hitler, Hindenburg signed a decree that made it easier for the government to crack down on Communists. That certainly happened, as police and SA men attacked and arrested anyone they suspected of being a Red (a Communist). The decree opened the door for Hitler too to claim that Germany was under attack from outside.

But what the decree really did was take away most of the rights and liberties that the German Republic had given its citizens since the end of the empire, following the war. Good-bye, freedom of the press. Good-bye, political rallies. Good-bye, the ability to speak out against the government. This decree was a disaster for democracy. The SA took full advantage and used their growing power to arrest and harass tens of thousands of people either they didn't like or who disagreed with them.

"I won't have to worry about justice," Hitler said in early March. "My mission is only to destroy and exterminate.... I shall lead the Brownshirts in this struggle to the death and my claws shall grasp your necks!"[48]

Things were going the Nazis' way, and the party would soon cement its power completely.

ALONG WITH THE SA, Hitler and the Nazis had established a military-like force called the Schutzstaffel (SS), which means "defense force." This group was led by a former soldier named

Heinrich Himmler, who would become one of Hitler's closest aides and an architect of death during World War II.

The SS and the SA put into prison the people they captured during the weeks and months following the end of civil liberties. The prisons soon grew into camps where thousands were stashed. Those camps became the models for the concentration camps where millions of Jews and others would be killed.

On March 23, 1933, Hitler demanded a new set of laws, called the Enabling Act, to grant him even more power. With the Reichstag now firmly in Nazi control, the vote was 441 to 94. The Enabling Act that was passed was the final piece of the puzzle for Hitler to take complete control. Though Hindenburg was still the president, Hitler ran the government. He could create a one-party state. The Nazis would soon be the only party anyone could belong to. That same month the Nazis opened the concentration camp at Dachau. It would not be the last such camp.

On April 1, Hitler went public again with his campaign against the Jews. He announced that a boycott was in effect for all German businesses owned by Jews. It was official government policy that citizens should not shop at such stores or use Jewish businesses. The Brownshirts were out in force to make sure people knew. A week later Hitler fired anyone who was Jewish working in the national government. The hateful process that would become the Holocaust was beginning in earnest.

AGAIN, WHY WAS this happening? What was Hitler's message that so many thought was the right one? There are lots of answers, but two main ones.

First, many people were happy to hear what Hitler was saying. At a time when many people had lost their jobs or lots of their money, they wanted someone to tell them everything would get better. Someone had to be blamed for the Germans' lot in life too. It was easy to simply say, *Sure, Hitler's right. It was the Jews . . . the Communists . . . the foreigners . . . the Gypsies. . . .* It was whomever he felt the most hatred for each time he spoke. He was building on decades of anger among the Germans for what had happened to them after the First World War (which, of course, they had started). Young people heard the stories from their parents about the great German empire, but those young people looked around and saw joblessness or low pay or hard-to-find food, and they said, *Hey, we should be great again.* Hitler said he would make that happen, as long as they all just did what he said. And from everything that we have seen or read about Hitler in those days, he had something about him that just made you want to listen and believe.

Second, the times were pretty scary. . . . The SA consisted of nearly five hundred thousand angry young men. When the Reichstag voted on the bill called the Enabling Act, SA forces surrounded the building in which the vote was held. (They chanted, "We want the bill—or fire and murder!")[49] SA soldiers, working not for the German military but for the Nazi Party, were almost completely unopposed. If they wanted to smash a shop owned by Jews, they did, and no one said anything, out of sheer fear. If they wanted to attack someone in the street, or break up another party's rally, or destroy a newspaper office for publishing anti-Nazi views . . . they just did it. The violence was public and clear, and anyone who opposed it risked their lives. The addition of the prison camps made the terror more real, because not only did people get beaten or assaulted, but now they were simply taken away. Scary? It certainly was.

11

NIGHT OF THE LONG KNIVES

What about the rest of the world? Why weren't they declaring that Hitler's actions were wrong? Well, they were, but not many people paid attention. People in America and Europe were writing about Hitler's anti-Jewish policies almost as soon as he took power, but the people writing were not as loud as Hitler. He was also a great liar. In the spring President Franklin Roosevelt, seeing things getting bad in Germany, called for all nations to declare that peace was the goal.

"Germany knows," Hitler said in response, "that in any military action in Europe, even if completely successful, the sacrifice would be out of all proportion to any possible gains."[50] The events of the coming years would prove that a lie. He was simply using his speeches to tell whoever was listening whatever that audience wanted to hear. Even when he led Germany in withdrawing from the League of Nations (a forerunner to the United Nations) in late 1933, it was not to simply protest that group's policies. It was to seem like a thoughtful and important leader. Meanwhile, he had his own terrible plan. And in the summer of 1934, he put it into action.

In this event Hitler showed—once again, some might say—just how truly awful and selfish he was. Since Hitler's earliest days with the Nazis, the SA had been a key part of his success. Called to action by his speeches, inspired by his words, they had tromped over civil liberties and been his powerful right arm. They had led the Beer Hall Putsch, they had surrounded the Reichstag. They had rounded up enemies and murdered thousands.

Now, as Hitler took the reins of government, he betrayed them. In order to gain control of the German army as well as the government, he had to appease the military leaders. (Unlike today, in those days military leadership was not necessarily under civilian political control.) The officers of the army hated the SA, which they felt was doing the job that the army should be doing, and was gaining power they felt was rightly theirs. For several months and at many meetings, Hitler negotiated a reduction of the SA's duties. They were given just a few small jobs and were now prevented from their freelance terror work. Then in June the members of the SA were all told to take a month off, whether they liked it or not.

In late June, Hitler became convinced that Ernst Röhm and the SA were going to revolt against him, his government, and the new rules.

So Hitler unleashed a night and a day of arrest, terror, and murder to simply do away with the SA leadership.

On June 30, Hitler and a group of armed supporters broke into Röhm's house as he slept. Armed with a pistol, Hitler himself told his longtime loyalist, "Ernst, you are under arrest."[51]

And so it began. He soon called Joseph Goebbels, his minister of propaganda, and said, "I gave the order to shoot those who were ringleaders in this treason."[52]

As night descended on Berlin and Munich and other cities, that order was carried out.

Former chancellor General von Schleicher. Killed.

Karl Ernst, one of the Munich SA leaders. Even as he said, "Heil Hitler!" he was killed.

And of course, finally, Ernst Röhm. Killed.

Dozens and dozens of people that Hitler believed, rightly or wrongly, were plotting against him or the party were murdered.

And on and on. In all, more than 150 people in key positions in the SA or in the Nazi Party itself were simply eliminated in what came to be called the Night of the Long Knives. The name came from a myth about the death of the comrades of the German hero Vortigen, but it also referred to the long reach of the plot, which was able to extend into many cities and cut out the parts of the SA that Hitler wanted to remove.

If people had not been not scared of Hitler before, these actions pushed their fear level off the charts. Millions realized that they had to join Hitler's group or die. If he could kill some of the most loyal and powerful people working tirelessly for him, what could the average German hope for? The average German Jew, however, was even more terrified.

A few weeks later Hitler arranged for the Reichstag to say that all the murders he had ordered were fine with them. No one was going to speak against him, now that he had shown his true colors. That summer Heinrich Himmler also took over command of the Gestapo. This was the military unit created by Hitler and the Nazis to serve as the party's in-house, heavily armed, ruthless police-like force. They would remain, along with the SS, the fist that Hitler used to crush any who opposed him.

And then things got really bad. On August 2 the great general and longtime president Hindenburg finally died at the age of eighty-seven. Without him to balance the insanity of Hitler, there was no stopping the former corporal. Hitler got a law passed almost instantly, without opposition, that said he was taking Hindenburg's place as president, while also remaining chancellor. For more than a decade he had been called the führer, or supreme leader, of the Nazi Party.

Now, he told Germany, he was the führer of the whole country.

12

HITLER IN CHARGE

One of the first things Hitler did was solidify his control of the Germany army. This was the group that had grumbled about the SA and in large part was the reason behind his Night of the Long Knives purge. Now that he was the supreme leader, he made himself their boss, whether they liked it or not. He made the leading generals and admirals—and eventually every member of the military—swear a personal oath not to Germany but to Hitler himself, supreme commander of the armed forces. He kept the generals in everyday charge of military, but it was clear who ran the show.

After a summer break, Hitler showcased all of his power and appeal at the annual Nuremberg rally, which was held every fall by the Nazi Party as a sort of cheerleading event to get the party faithful excited. The 1934 event exceeded every previous rally. Under the direction of an architect named Albert Speer, who would be a key part of many future Nazi events and buildings, tens of thousands of people worked to create a Nazi spectacle. People were trucked in from around the country and assigned jobs and places to march or stand. At events spread out over several days, Hitler gave speech after speech to adoring crowds. It was carefully arranged by his key associates to make him and the party look as good and as strong as possible. Vast hordes of people stood in perfect lines, dressed in black SS uniforms, the brown shirts of the SA, or other uniforms. They lined up on enormous squares in front of huge stages covered with red-and-black swastika banners. The main speeches were made under a huge stone eagle with a hundred-foot-wide wingspan.

Among the people watching, amazed at this mesmerizing

spectacle was an American journalist. William Shirer was among the first outside Germany to really understand the depth of Hitler's power and the love that his followers felt for him.

"Every word dropped by Hitler seemed like an inspired word from on high," Shirer wrote. "Man's—or at least the German's—critical faculty [ability to think] is swept away at such moments, and every lie pronounced is accepted as high truth itself."[53]

Even then Shirer and outsiders could see that what Hitler was preaching was not really the truth but the truth as Hitler saw it and proclaimed it.

Almost every moment of the event was captured on film by a director named Leni Riefenstahl, personally hired by Hitler for the event. The film she made, called *Triumph of the Will*, provided a wide audience with their first glimpse—clips were shown around Europe and in the US eventually—of just what Hitler could do while giving a speech. His wild arm movements, the spit flying from his mouth, the voice that rose higher and higher as he got angrier and angrier—to outsiders he seemed to be a madman. To many Germans he was becoming like a god.

Hitler knew the power that images had to move people. To make sure that his massive rallies at Nuremberg, and later at the 1936 Berlin Olympics, were captured on film, he turned to an unlikely director. Leni Riefenstahl was a German film actress who had caught Hitler's attention. After some early work, she made her first major movie about the 1934 rally, called *Triumph of the Will*. In 1936 she made *Olympia*, about that year's Olympic Games.

Her life and career were controversial. Though many admired her groundbreaking camera work—she used unusual angles, slow motion, and special filters, among other techniques—her subject matter, of course, was not admired. She was accused of glorifying Hitler and the Nazis. Still, the two films are still regarded as masterpieces of the art of propaganda. Riefenstahl lived a long life after the war, trying to continue to make art even as many turned their backs on her due to her Nazi connections. She died in 2003 at the age of 101.

To Jewish Germans, Hitler was proving to be the devil.

And then Hitler made another bold move. The Treaty of Versailles that had ended World War I was still in force. It was one of the things that had set Hitler on his course to restore Germany to what he felt was its rightful place. But the treaty placed limits on the size of the German military. Knowing that he needed a larger army and more weapons to meet his goals, in March 1935, Hitler simply dissolved the treaty. He did not have the power to do this, of course. Both parties of a treaty have to agree to change it. Hitler, as usual, didn't care.

While his underlings rapidly worked to build a new and larger Germany army, Hitler turned his attention, once again, to the Jews.

In late 1935, Hitler directed the Reichstag to create laws putting more limits on Germany's Jewish citizens. Known as the Nuremberg Laws because they were signed not long after that year's Nazi rally at Nuremberg, these decrees were the harshest yet. The laws banned marriage between Germans and Jews. Jews could no longer hire Germans to work for them, nor could Jews display or use the German flag. It basically made

German Jews, some of whose families had been in the country for many generations, into noncitizens.

Surprisingly, these laws, as harsh as they look today, did not meet with much protest. Certainly few Jewish people could object, because, of course, that would be even worse than breaking one of the laws. But many Jewish people in Germany felt that this was at least the signal they needed. They didn't like the lines that were drawn, but at least they had clear lines. They wanted to stay in Germany, so many just felt they could somehow adapt and muddle through. For more than two years that's pretty much what they did.

However, away from the eyes of the public, another menace was growing. Those Jews who were found to have broken laws were taken away. Also removed was anyone who spoke out against Hitler. Even making Nazi jokes was a quick way to get arrested. Where did all the people go? To concentration camps. Thanks to Himmler and the SS, the Nazis were simply packing all the people they didn't want into large camps. This was not jail or prison, where someone might be sent after a legal process and provided with food and shelter while serving a sentence. Instead the Nazis packed people in with little regard for their safety or comfort. It was strict punishment. It would not be the last time the Nazis did this.

In the spring of 1936, Hitler, now in charge of a massive army, decided to make a bold move. A portion of Germany on its western border with France was called the Rhineland. The Versailles Treaty said that no arms or soldiers from Germany could be in that area. It was demilitarized. France actually had troops ready to make sure that remained true. But on March 7, 1936, Hitler directed units of the army to march into the Rhineland in direct violation of the Versailles Treaty.

And then he waited . . . impatiently. Why? Because if France or England or the other Allies from World War I decided to fight back, would his brand-new army be able to win? Would a defeat at this point harm his rule?

Years later Hitler wrote, "The forty-eight hours after the march into the Rhineland were the most nerve-racking in my life. If the French had marched into the Rhineland, we would have had to withdraw with our tail between our legs." Historian Ian Kershaw also noted about the Rhineland event, "This proved the last chance, short of war, for Western democracies to stop Hitler in his tracks. Why did they not do so? After all [as it turned out], only a small German force advanced into the Rhineland, and with orders to retreat if challenged."[54] France did not know that, of course, but its inaction in the face of a German move was one that the führer noted with glee.

Indeed, as German troops marched in, nothing happened. French troops retreated. England grumbled but did nothing. No other European country had any interest in more war. The United States remained quiet as well.

In May 1936, Hitler addressed the Reichstag and, like a good politician, told Europe what it wanted to hear. "Germany wants peace . . . None of us means to threaten anybody,"[55] Hitler declared. Of course he didn't mean a word of it, as things turned out.

Germany, led by Hitler, was on the march to war . . . again.

13

THE BERLIN OLYMPICS

One of the driving forces in Hitler's mind for the move into the Rhineland and many of the other moves he made is summed up in a German word: Lebensraum. It means "living space." To Hitler it meant much more than that. Since Germany's loss in World War I, the nation had actually shrunk. Hitler could not stand this. He believed that it was the right of the German people to expand and that they needed more land to make room for their growing population. And he believed it was his job to make sure Germany got that land, even if the territory belonged to someone else.

The Rhineland was the first step, but he had many others in mind as 1936 rolled on.

But first he had to go to the Olympics.

Berlin had been awarded the summer Games in 1931. By the time the actual event rolled around, Germany had been taken over by the Nazis. So they took over the Olympics, too. Nazi banners flew at the events, a huge stadium was built for key sports, and all of Berlin was focused on showing the world the strength of the Nazis.

Jews, of course, were banned from being on Germany's team. This, finally, created an international controversy because of the Olympics spotlight. Countries taking part protested that this was not right, as the Games were supposed to be free of politics and open to all. In the United States a strong movement rose to boycott the Games and not even send a team. One American sports leader said that sending was like giving "American moral and financial support to the Nazi regime, which is opposed to all that Americans hold dearest."[56]

However, the man who ran the US Olympic Committee, Avery Brundage, was a longtime anti-Semite. He didn't really mind Hitler's policies. He had been wined and dined on a visit to Germany in 1934. He was also a very powerful leader. In the end, he won a vote to send the team.

The Games were a Nazi propaganda event from the moment they opened. Berlin was scrubbed to perfection, though visitors saw many anti-Jewish signs and placards. At the opening ceremony on August 1, nation after nation paraded past Hitler, as the head of state overseeing the Games. Some nations made the Nazi salute; others did not. Each flag dipped as it passed him, except one. Though born in Berlin, Al Jochim had become an American citizen. A gymnast, he was chosen to carry the US flag in the parade. As he passed Hitler, he pointedly did not dip the flag. It was seen as a great insult by Germans, but Americans were thrilled.

Another American had a big impact on the Games and on Hitler. Along with Jews, Nazis placed people of African descent many rungs below Aryans on the human ladder. Africans were seen as secondary humans, uncivilized and unworthy. The United States team included nineteen African Americans. Hitler was particularly focused on his Aryan-led team defeating these black athletes. One of those athletes instead made history in the face of Nazi hatred.

Jesse Owens, a track athlete from Ohio, won four gold medals—three in sprints and one in the long jump, while setting three world records. By the end of his time on the track, Owens was cheered even by the German fans. He was mobbed when he went out in Berlin. His talent and success had, for a moment, overcome hatred. Owens became an international superstar. Hitler was not happy about that. A legend grew that Hitler refused to shake Owens's hand after the American won his events, but Hitler actually did not visit with any winners except a couple of Germans the day before Owens's first win.

Germany did win the Games. Its athletes captured eighty-nine medals, more than the American team's fifty-six. However, the presence of the Nazis and Hitler at these Games was overshadowed by Owens's success.

At the 1936 Olympics one man showed the world that Hitler's ideals of the Aryan master race were false. American track star Jesse Owens, already holder of several world records, won four gold medals in a stunning week of success that put the lie to Hitler's claims.

Owens had grown up very poor in Alabama, but his athletic skills helped him rise from those beginnings, especially after his family moved to Cleveland before he started high school. At Ohio State he once set or tied four world records in forty-five minutes.

The idea of America's sending a team to Nazi Germany in 1936 was very controversial. Many objected, and only a very close vote—and the forcible leadership of the anti-Semitic head of the US Olympic Committee, Avery Brundage—let the team travel. The irony, of course, was that as an African American, Owens was a second-class citizen at home, but in the Olympics he came to represent all of America.

As Hitler watched, Owens won the 100 meters event. A rumor at the time said that Hitler snubbed the winner by refusing to shake his hand. Though Hitler was clearly not pleased, there was no ceremony planned where such a snub could take place. Owens then won the 200 meters and the long jump, beating German Aryan competitors in each. The American capped it off by running with his countrymen to win the 4x100-meter relay race. Owens remains one of America's most famous Olympians and a symbol of the world's standing up to Hitler's evil.

When the Games ended, Hitler once again turned his attention to Lebensraum. His growing army needed some work, and he needed another victory. Hitler turned his eyes to the south . . . to a familiar country . . . Austria.

14

EXPANDING GERMANY

Throughout 1937, Hitler continued to pull the reins of power in Germany tighter and tighter. The Nuremberg Laws were being used to fill the concentration camps—along with Dachau, Buchenwald had opened—with Jews and other "undesirables." Hitler also chose new generals to lead the armed forces—generals loyal only to him, to replace the holdovers from before, who had until then held on to their ranks.

Also in 1937, Hitler moved to solidify a relationship with the one European leader who had no problem with his actions. In Italy, Benito Mussolini was essentially doing the same thing that Hitler was doing in Germany. Mussolini's Fascist Party had run Italy since 1922. He had taken over Libya, Ethiopia, and Somalia in a bid to create a new Italian empire. Fascists were nearly as repressive as Nazis, and Mussolini was basically a dictator. He was known as "Il Duce."

Hitler invited Il Duce to visit Germany in 1937 to make sure that Italy would not bother Germany as it planned its expansion. Mussolini already had praised Hitler. He had invented the term that the two countries would be called during wartime: the Axis powers. The Italian leader said that the future of Europe would spin on the axis of the two nations. Hitler put on a huge show to demonstrate to Mussolini how much the führer was admired in Germany. More than a million people lined a parade route in Berlin. Both men gave speeches, and when the Italian left, Hitler knew that he had made a firm friend.

In March 1938, totally confident of success, Hitler pulled off his biggest land grab to date. And it was a land he was very familiar with—Austria. He tried without success to get the government of that nation to simply agree to join Germany under Nazi rule. He even brought the Austrian chancellor, Kurt von Schuschnigg, to the führer's retreat at Berchtesgaden, high in the German Alps. There Hitler bullied and shouted at Schuschnigg. He threatened Austria with bloodshed and war; he paraded his generals in their medals in front of the frightened Austrian. Hitler basically told the man, *Give me your country or else.*

Hitler knew that he had the backing of a party in Austria that was attracted to the ideals of the Nazis, since many Austrians, like Hitler, also considered themselves Germans at heart. Schuschnigg left without really agreeing to give up, though Hitler thought he had. When the Austrian chancellor returned to Austria, he tried to speak out against the planned takeover, but it didn't work. Mobs of Austrians, most with German roots, who supported Hitler took to the streets, demanding that Hitler take over. Other people in the country were terribly frightened and the nation teetered on the brink of collapse. In the end, negotiations didn't work, so Hitler went with brute force. On March 12, 1938, he sent his army into Austria. They were met with almost no resistance. A month later Austrians "voted"—while Germans literally pointed guns at them—to sign a pact with Germany. The event is known as the Anschluss, a German word meaning "union" or "connection."

Hitler went to Vienna shortly thereafter, an amazing return for the man who had once had to eat at soup kitchens in the same city. He stayed at the finest hotels, where one report says he had once worked for pennies, shoveling snow. While Hitler dined in splendor, Nazis and others in Austria joined in the ongoing German attacks on Jews. Austrian Jews were attacked in the streets, were kicked out of their homes, and saw their businesses wrecked. Many were simply arrested and taken away, to a new concentration camp that had sprung up in Austria almost overnight.

Hitler was not done creating more Lebensraum for his people. Next he turned his focus to an area of nearby Czechoslovakia, to the east. Part of that country, called the Sudetenland, was home to many ethnic Germans, and Hitler wanted to add it to a growing Germany. Instead of simply taking it, he got the rest of Europe to give it to him. Europe's desperate fear of another world war was playing right into Hitler's hands. He demanded a meeting in Munich, at which he claimed the right to take the Sudetenland without compensating Czechoslovakia. France, England, and Italy simply signed off on the agreement. Notably, no one from Czechoslovakia was invited to the conference that led to the signing. Hitler rolled the Sudetenland into his growing nation.

Hitler got away with this blatant theft partly because of a man named Neville Chamberlain, prime minister of Great Britain. Few leaders have ever been as afraid of war as Chamberlain was. His actions in this crisis and in the coming months would brand him as one of the most ineffectual politicians ever.

Like the Austrian leader, Chamberlain was summoned to Berchtesgaden, Germany, to meet with Hitler, who proceeded to use the same tactics that had worked before. Hitler talked and talked and yelled and ranted, though with a slightly softer edge. He was trying to convince Chamberlain that the Germans who lived in the Sudetenland were being persecuted by Czech and Slovak majorities. Hitler claimed he was just helping them find their own homeland. It was a farce, of course, and he was more than ready to invade to get what he wanted, no matter what anyone else thought. But getting the British and other Western nations to go along with it would give Hitler even more power. Chamberlain at first did not agree, but then saw that giving Hitler what he wanted was the only way to prevent war, or so he thought. His appeasement of Hitler turned out very badly.

As evidence of how much Chamberlain was both afraid of war and fooled by Hitler, after returning home, Chamberlain said, "In spite of the hardness and ruthlessness I thought I saw in his face, I got the impression that here was a man who could be relied upon when he had given his word."[57]

Chamberlain was clearly wrong, and it was proved days later when Hitler simply said that the agreement about the Sudetenland was no longer enough. He wanted the whole country.

That really rocked the democracies of Western Europe. Here, finally, was Hitler lining up his guns to take over an independent country that really didn't want him there. In answer to Hitler's threats, France began sending troops to its border with Germany. The Czechoslovakian army got ready for a fight. London itself got ready for war, while the British Navy prepared to head out to sea. What they had all feared was almost happening, and seeing that, Chamberlain again looked for a way out. Taking Hitler at his word about staying out of Czechoslovakia, he agreed to let the Germans take over the Sudetenland. He returned to Germany and led the nations meeting in Munich to sign over the Sudetenland, which has been Hitler's aim all along. Chamberlain returned to England and declared that he had achieved "peace in our time."[58] Falser words were never spoken. Privately, of course, Hitler didn't think much of the Allies arrayed against him, calling them "little worms."

After all of the embarrassment and mistakes, Chamberlain was forced to admit that he'd been swindled. "Hitler is the commonest little swine I have ever encountered," he said. In the following years, Chamberlain's appeasement came to be regarded as a huge turning point in Hitler's drive to war.

Hitler had once again proven that he was relentless in his desire for land and power, ruthless in his willingness to lie or bully to get his way, and desperate to reach his goals. At several points he said to associates that he wanted to get things taken care of soon. He was almost fifty years old, he said, and he didn't know how much more time he had. Hitler's hurry to war continued, but first he had some things at home to take care of.

15

KRISTALLNACHT

A series of small events in early November 1938 followed the previous decade of larger events, and all added up to the worst night yet for Jews living under Nazi rule.

The Enabling Act and the Nuremberg Laws had already made life very difficult, if not impossible, for German Jews. Similar rules in Austria and the Sudetenland expanded the danger to Jews in those areas. The hatred for Jews was growing month by month, year by year, with less and less connection to any rational reason. It was simply pure hate.

On November 7 a Polish Jew named Herschel Grynszpan, whose family had been kicked out of Germany, reached his breaking point. Living in Paris and seeing the troubles brewing in Germany, he had tried to get his family to safety in Poland, without success. The family was stuck at the border, with nowhere to go. Desperate and enraged, Grynszpan went to the Germany embassy in Paris and attacked a man he had met there. Grynszpan shot Ernst vom Rath and killed him.

Two days later, on November 9, vom Rath died. That was the fifteenth anniversary of the Beer Hall Putsch. Nazis were gathered together in cities throughout Germany to celebrate the anniversary. Hitler himself was in Munich. As his dinner began, he got word that vom Rath had died. Hitler and Goebbels thought that this event could be used to their advantage. With Hitler's permission, Goebbels quickly spread the word that it would be fine with the leader if Nazis struck back.

In fact, vom Rath's death was just an excuse to stoke a fire that had been smoldering for years. Starting in Munich and spreading quickly around the nation after news was spread by telephone, that night Nazi groups, led by the Hitler Youth and the SA, went crazy. Nazi leaders did nothing to stop them. It was not planned ahead of time, but it was clearly approved at the highest levels. Goebbels said that evening, "The Führer has decided that . . . demonstrations should not be prepared or organized by the Party, but insofar as they erupt spontaneously, they are not to be hampered."[59]

For hours, claiming to be protesting the death of vom Rath, Nazis young and old stalked the streets of the cities. They smashed any Jewish business they could find and attacked Jews in the streets. More than two hundred synagogues—Jewish houses of worship—were burned. Jewish cemeteries were attacked, with rioters knocking over tombstones and crypts. More than seven thousand businesses were looted. More than thirty thousand Jewish men were arrested for no crime other than their heritage and beliefs. Though an official number can never be known, more than two thousand people may have died that night or shortly after.

It was a horrible night. In the firelight of torches, the broken glass covering street after street glittered and sparkled and gave the event its name—Kristallnacht, the Night of Crystal.

If Chamberlain's appeasement was the international turning point in Nazi rule, then Kristallnacht was the launch moment for what became the Holocaust.

WHAT WAS THE rest of the world doing as this happened? Finally they were taking notice. For half a decade Hitler and the Nazis had been smashing the rights, lives, and property of its Jewish citizens, with little argument from outside the nation. Some groups in both the United States and Great Britain cheered, in fact, joining the Nazis in their anti-Semitism.

But Kristallnacht was too much. As the news got out and the pictures and stories spread around the world, the Western nations laid into Germany . . . with words. The United States brought its ambassador to Germany home, a move considered a real slap in the face in normal times. Newspapers and radio commentators in the United States, Britain, France, and elsewhere condemned the violence and destruction.

President Franklin Roosevelt, who had been mostly silent

as the Nazis had taken power, finally spoke out. "I myself could scarcely believe that such things could occur in a twentieth-century civilization," he said.[60]

Nazi Germany was finally—finally—being recognized for the violent, racist bully that it had become under the leadership of Hitler.

Did Hitler and Germany care, however? No, they did not. The appeasement that had let Hitler take Austria, the Rhineland, and the Sudetenland led him to believe that he could do whatever he wanted. Even if international forces objected, they were not ready to back up their words with action. And Hitler was not afraid to act.

In the days after Kristallnacht, as Jews in Germany tried to pick up the pieces of their broken lives or simply get out of the country any way they could, Germany cracked down even further. New laws and rules kicked Jewish children out of school and kicked adults out of every profession. Jews could not drive or go to any public events, such as theaters or movies.

To top it off, German authorities blamed the Jews for the whole mess of Kristallnacht. They even fined the Jewish population one billion marks for the damage. Hermann Göring summed up the Nazi point of view at a meeting announcing the fine. "I shall close the meeting with these words," he said. "German Jewry shall, as punishment for their abominable crimes, et cetera, have to make a contribution [of] one billion marks. That will work. The swine won't commit another murder. Incidentally, I would like to say that I would not like to be a Jew in Germany."

Not long after, Hitler spoke to a small gathering of Nazi Party officials. He was recorded there saying something that he had been thinking for a long time but had not really spelled out in so many words. After ranting against the Jewish bankers and Jewish Bolsheviks (Communists) as usual, he added a frightening new answer to his problem. He said that if the Jews forced another world war, it would lead to "the annihilation of the Jewish race in Europe."[61]

As 1939 began, German Jews faced a threat to their existence such as few other people ever had before. Within a year the rest of the world would face that threat as well.

16

THE EVE OF WAR

Hitler began 1939 with an eye toward lining up a few more pieces before he called for the war he knew had to happen in order for his dreams to come true. At home his military grew and grew. Led by Göring, German industry had been pouring out weapons, tanks, trucks, and ammunition as part of a four-year plan that Hitler had announced back in 1936. Throughout the latter 1930s the Hitler Youth had evolved into a huge German army, desperately loyal to the führer they had grown up worshipping.

The SS and the Gestapo had an iron grip on Germany itself; no one was brave enough to speak against Hitler. The issue of smashing the Jews was clearly settled; German law and national opinion was quickly turning Jewish lives into hell.

Looking outside Germany for his next move, Hitler sent his troops to easily take over the rest of Czechoslovakia, expanding on his foothold in the Sudetenland. The different ethnic groups that had combined to make the new Czechoslovak nation after World War I got no help from outside their country, and the Nazi empire grew again.

For his part Hitler reveled in the new addition. He made a personal visit to Prague, the capital, riding at the front of a line of army trucks. He toasted the victory in Prague's hotels and restaurants, gleeful that yet again he had done exactly what he wanted to do and no one had tried to stop him. Not Great Britain, not France, not the United States.

To continue his march toward full Lebensraum, Hitler had to make sure that outside leaders would not stand in his way. He knew that eventually Great Britain and France would have to fight back against German aggression, and he was confident his forces could handle them. But Italy, to the south, was a nation also led by a brutal ruler, and he wanted to build on his already existing friendship with Mussolini to ensure that Germany could do what it wanted. Farther to the east the Soviet Union, by then the world's largest country, loomed. Hitler hated the Soviets and their leader, Joseph Stalin. But he knew that he could not beat them in a fight at that point; there were too many things that could go wrong there that would derail his plans. So as 1939 rolled on, Hitler moved the pieces on his personal chess board.

AFTER SEIZING CZECHOSLOVAKIA, Hitler made another demand for land, as he had with the Sudetenland. He said that Germany should reclaim an area now in Poland called East Prussia. The Germans wanted to remove from Polish control a strip of land that gave Poland its only access to the sea at the free city of Danzig. Danzig was home to several million ethnic Germans who wanted back into Germany. The Versailles Treaty had set up the unusual geographical arrangement. Germany had been forced to give up the strip of land as punishment after World War I. Hitler wanted to change that agreement.

This verbal attack on Poland was, finally, the last straw for England. Chamberlain's feeble hope that they could get Hitler to stop had vanished. Politicians and citizens were outraged at what the Hitler was doing. With his threat against Poland, a country with no real German ethnic ties and one that had great relations with England, Hitler had pushed too far.

"In the event of any action, which clearly threatens Polish Independence," Chamberlain said to Parliament, "... His Majesty's Government would feel themselves bound at once to lend the Polish Government all support."[62]

With that threat hanging in the air, Hitler pushed back with a visible threat of his own. He invited European leaders to a birthday party—his own. He turned fifty as a display of Germany military might paraded by him in Berlin. Anti-aircraft guns rolled by on flatbed trucks. Tanks and artillery drove ahead, along with regiment after regiment of soldiers marching in the approved goose-stepping Nazi way, all while fleets of planes roared past overhead. It was a devastating spectacle, witnessed by the diplomats of many other governments. It was physical evidence of the complete hold that Hitler had on Germany and its people.

A biographer noted that this poem was taught to children in all German schools.

> *Adolf Hitler is our savior, our hero*
> *He is the noblest being in the whole wide world.*
> *For Hitler we live,*
> *For Hitler we die.*
> *Our Hitler is our Lord, who rules a brave new world.* [63]

IN MAY 1939, Hitler took another step toward creating his own new world when he signed the Pact of Steel with Italy, which bound the two countries together in a military alliance. Both sides pledged to come to the other's aid in case of war, "with all its military forces on land, on sea, and in the air." [64]

Hitler took a short break in early August to greet an old friend. August Kubizek, the man who had been one of the first to listen to Hitler's rantings back when they were teenagers, attended the opera with the führer. He brought postcards for Hitler to sign for his friends, and Hitler and he went for a walk in the garden where their hero, composer Richard Wagner, was buried. It was a rare moment of calm in a stormy year.

The next dark cloud came from the east. As Hitler finalized plans to attack Poland, he wanted to make sure he had one more possible threat bottled up. Joseph Stalin had ruled the Soviet Union with brutality and fear since 1929. He still called himself and his nation Communist, but they acted like anything but. Stalin spent most of the 1930s killing people he thought would get in his way, among them Jews and Communist Party members, but also other ethnic groups as well as many members of his own army. As a person who had spoken out threateningly for years about Communists and Bolsheviks, Hitler was certainly no friend of Stalin. But Hitler wanted to make sure that the Soviet leader was not an enemy, either. He tried to do the same thing with Stalin that he had done with the leaders of Poland, Austria, and Czechoslovakia. Using a combination of talk, bullying, and lies, he and his associates maneuvered Stalin into a pact.

AFTER MANY WEEKS of negotiations, mostly led by Hitler's foreign minister, Joachim von Ribbentrop, Germany and the Soviet Union signed a nonaggression pact on August 23. Essentially it said that Germany would not attack the Soviet Union and vice versa. It also included a huge trade deal that would send money and goods from Germany to the Soviet Union. A secret part of the agreement said that the Soviet Union could end up with chunks of land in Eastern Europe in return for letting Germany do as it pleased everywhere else.

The world was truly shocked. It was as if dogs and cats had signed an agreement saying they would never fight again. Hitler's Germany and Stalin's Soviet Union had been seen as deadly enemies. With this pact, the world saw, Germany was totally free to wage whatever war it wanted.

(It is interesting to note what Hitler thought of Stalin. Hitler admired the Soviet for his ferocity and his lack of fear about killing rivals. But when Ribbentrop came back to Germany, having taken close-up pictures of Stalin on Hitler's orders, Hitler checked the images carefully. He said he was looking for evidence around Stalin's ears that the leader was not Jewish. There is no real way to tell this, of course, but Hitler believed there was. And he was pleased to "see" that Stalin was not Jewish.)

With the Soviet Union now on the sidelines, and with Hitler believing that England would cave again ("The English will leave the Poles in the lurch as they did the Czechs,"[65] he told his aides), Hitler finally gave the order he had been waiting to give for months.

On September 1, 1939, German ships started lobbing shells onto Polish forces in Danzig. At the border with Germany, bombers flew overhead into Polish air space. Artillery weapons blasted shell after shell into Polish land. Tanks and men—as many as 1.5 million over the coming days—followed in a massive wave.

World War II had begun.

17

BLITZKRIEG!

While German forces poured into Poland, Great Britain tried one more time to talk Hitler out of his actions. A final deal was rejected, and on September 3, Chamberlain went on the radio to tell the world that Great Britain was now at war with Germany. France announced the same thing soon after. Owing to the pact with Germany, Stalin and the Soviet Union did nothing. In America, Roosevelt called on Hitler to avoid bombing cities and civilians, but otherwise America was not in this fight . . . yet.

The German Army marched forward, knocking aside Polish troops easily. The Germans were using a type of warfare that Hitler had come up with that would prove to be a devastating weapon all its own. Instead of slowly working their way into territory, German troops moved fast. They were engaging in blitzkrieg, which means "lightning war." They didn't try to gain and hold territory a little at a time. Hitler had seen how useless that strategy was in World War I. He did not want his troops stuck in trenches and mud. His armies were about speed, fear, and attack.

German bombers blew up Polish airplanes before they could even get into the air. Huge forces of tanks and men attacked one point in a Polish line and then swarmed through, spreading out so that the Polish troops soon found themselves surrounded. Hitler himself visited the battlefront to observe his plan and his army in action. People watching him noted that he no longer wore a business suit or even the brown uniform of his Nazi Party. As he peered through binoculars toward the battle, he was dressed in the gray-and-black uniform of a commander in the Germany Army.

The former mud-covered, gas-attacked Austrian-turned-German corporal was now the most powerful—and most important—soldier in Europe.

Hitler watched from the front and later from back in Berlin as Polish cities fell in days. The capital of Warsaw held out a bit longer, but it too was overwhelmed.

In September, Soviet troops did take part on the side of the Germans. They moved into eastern Poland unopposed.

As the world then saw to its horror, the Soviet-German pact had even greater repercussions than they had thought it would. Later in the year, Stalin's troops would pour into Finland. Within weeks the Soviet Union had greatly expanded its western borders. Far to the west, England and France were almost powerless.

As 1939 moved into the fall, Hitler once again gave a speech designed to convince both Germans and the Western European allies arrayed against Germany that he actually wanted peace. When England did not immediately agree to a peace settlement (since, of course, Hitler didn't want any such thing), Nazi officials could tell the German people, *Look, we're just defending ourselves against those English people*. The majority of Germany's forces were still in Poland, and the military leaders were afraid that Hitler's blitzkrieg strategy could not be sustained.

In fact, there were enough people in high positions in the army who did not like what Hitler was doing that a plot was undertaken to kill him. Many thought he was moving too fast, but he had hurt hundreds of thousands of ordinary people too. One of them, Georg Elser, figured out how to plant a bomb near the spot where Hitler would be speaking. The bomb was timed to explode about halfway through the speech. However, at the last moment Hitler wrapped up early and walked away to a waiting train. The bomb did go off and killed and wounded many people. Once again, though, Hitler walked away unhurt.

Hitler would later say that an astrologer—Hitler believed greatly in signs from the stars—had told him that something like this would happen around this date in November. After he heard about the bomb, Hitler said, "The fact that I left [the station] earlier than usual is a corroboration [sign] of Providence's intention to let me reach my goal."[66] Every time it seemed like he might fail or be stopped but instead succeeded, Hitler gained more inner strength and conviction. No one could kill him, he thought, and no one could make him do anything he didn't want to do. His war plans continued.

FRANCE, MEANWHILE, LOOKED to be in good shape for a war. It had four times as many soldiers available to fight as the Germans had. Plus the French army was able to settle in behind a line of defense set up years before. The Maginot Line was supposed to be the thing that would stop any German attack. Its fortresses, guns, and walls were seen as unbeatable. But the line went only so far north. In that direction was the open flat country of the Netherlands, Belgium, and Luxembourg, the Low Countries. And tank drivers love low countries.

After a winter of building up his forces inside Germany and establishing total control over Poland to the east, Hitler welcomed spring 1940 with a new attack to the west in April. First he sent ships filled with men and tanks via the North Sea to back up forces coming from Germany by land. British warships tried to help, and they also sent thousands of troops. The British navy did destroy many German ships, but it was not enough. Next Hitler sent thousands of tanks roaring into the Low Countries, while also taking over Denmark to the north in days. German troops also poured off ships that had crossed the Baltic Sea to Norway. The Norwegians held on for more than two months, but soon they, too, had to give up.

On May 10, Hitler set his boldest plan yet in motion. Raining bombs down from the sky on major Dutch and Belgian cities, Germany's forces swarmed over the Low Countries north of the Maginot Line. The queen of Holland was rescued by British ships. Within days the Netherlands, Belgium, and even tiny Luxembourg were controlled by Germany. As France saw what was happening, it rushed troops and weapons north to help. That left parts of the Maginot Line less well-manned . . . just as Hitler had anticipated.

"When the news came that the enemy was advancing along the whole front," Hitler reportedly said, "I could have wept for joy; they'd fallen into the trap!"[67]

One of the largest gatherings of tanks and men ever pounced on this weakness and within days had rolled through northern France and reached the edges of Paris.

The German advance was a total rout, a blitzkrieg domination of country after country. Hitler's Lebensraum, his desire for revenge against the West, and his need for power and control . . . he had it all.

England had sent hundreds of thousands of men across the English Channel to help in the fight, but it was too little too late.

In less than a year Hitler had taken over most of Western Europe. No one had the power to stop him. He was waging a kind of war that no one had seen. It was not about holding territory or gaining resources. It was simply about overtaking, smashing, and spreading fear.

By late May 1940 nearly all the forces fighting back against Hitler—English, French, Dutch, Belgian, and others—had been pinned in one small area on the northwest coast of France. It was a disaster.

18

TAKING FRANCE

More than three hundred thousand men were crammed along the coast near the French city of Dunkirk. Hitler's tanks idled just miles away . . . but did not advance. Hitler, encouraged by Göring, his air force (Luftwaffe) commander, decided to let planes rather than the tanks finish off the trapped Allied forces. It was a rare mistake.

While British and German airplanes battled in the skies overhead, and bad weather kept planes from flying on other days, one of history's most famous rescues was accomplished. Nearly one thousand civilian ships—fishermen, yachts, pleasure craft, ferries, and more—joined with British Navy ships to take all those soldiers off the beach and out of harm's way. In just a few days Dunkirk was evacuated. Hitler's forces still captured thousands of French soldiers, but the bravery of the rescuers at Dunkirk gave the British people good news and instant heroes as the new war began.

Still angered by the misstep at Dunkirk, Hitler ordered his land forces to finish the job in France. Starting from the north, they rolled through France almost unopposed.

By the middle of June, what all of France and most of Europe had feared—German occupation—had come to pass. A red-and-black Nazi swastika flag fluttered above the highest points of Paris. The city, surrounded, was forced to surrender on June 14. Hitler sped to the city to take possession of what was to that point his greatest treasure.

The City of Light, long a symbol of culture and love, had always been for Hitler a city with very different meanings. It was the French who had beaten him and Germany back in World

War I. It had been the French, in his mind, who had set up the Treaty of Versailles that had crushed Germany. So now he had a chance for revenge. In a moment that he surely loved, he forced French officials to sign surrender documents in a familiar spot—the actual railroad car where, back in 1918, the Germans had signed similar documents. Hitler had ordered it removed from the museum where it had been kept. An entire wall of the museum building had to be torn down to get it out. To rewrite history Hitler let nothing get in his way. As the documents were signed, Hitler achieved his greatest revenge, forcing his most hated enemy to kneel before him.

American journalist William Shirer was among the witnesses. He wrote afterward about Hitler's attitude. "It was grave, solemn, yet brimming with revenge. There was also in it, as in his springy step, a note of the triumphant conqueror, the defier of the world."[68]

A few days later Hitler toured Paris. He stopped at the opera and thought about seeing his beloved Wagner performed there. A famous photo of him was taken with the Eiffel Tower in the background. He went to the tomb of Napoléon, perhaps the only other man who had ever "owned" as much of Europe as Hitler now did. Over and over he told aides how his longed-for career in art had been inspired by Paris long ago. He pointed out the beautiful buildings and famous views. He had told his troops not to bomb or wreck the city, because he wanted to preserve it and see it for himself. The streets, meanwhile, were nearly empty. Parisians were scared and did not know what would come next.

What this meant for the rest of France, and especially French Jews, played out in the next few weeks and months. As he had when taking over Poland, Czechoslovakia, and the Low Countries, Hitler expanded his anti-Jewish policies to his newly won lands. Nazis worked with local officials to find and "collect" Jews and others undesirables. Trains soon started leaving France for concentration camps in the east. Similar trains would run from Holland, Belgium, and Denmark. The familiar six-pointed yellow star that German Jews were forced to wear would eventually be seen in Paris, Amsterdam, and Brussels.

Meanwhile, in Poland a similar campaign was under way, but with even more deadly results. Along with arresting or simply killing Jews in Poland, the Nazis ended higher education, in order to make sure that few people could have the knowledge to stop them. At one point Himmler instructed that, "The non-German population of the eastern territories must not receive any education higher than that of an elementary school with four grades. The objective of this elementary school must simply be to teach simple arithmetic up to 500 at the most, how to write one's name, and to teach that it is God's commandment to be obedient to the Germans and to be honest, hard working, and well-behaved. I consider it unnecessary to teach reading."[69]

The Nazis also kidnapped Polish children they believed to be Aryans from their Polish parents, such as those with blond hair or blue eyes. For Jews, ghettos (segregated living areas) were set up in major Polish cities. The terror behind the army was spreading.

Back in France, Hitler and Germany officially took over the northern half of that nation. In a desperate bid to hold on to some of its territory, France worked out a deal. Under control of Marshal Henri-Philippe Pétain, a separate French government would take charge of the south of France. It was led from a town called Vichy, so the "nation" was Vichy France. Vichy cooperated with the Nazis and let them take away whomever they wanted.

In the east another ominous sign of the future was the opening of Auschwitz, a concentration camp in Poland that would become the site of Hitler's deadliest move yet to rid the world of Jews.

In Italy, Mussolini watched in surprise as Hitler attacked and attacked. Though he was Hitler's ally, even he believed that this was too much too soon. However, as he saw the success, he decided to jump in. In June he sent Italian forces into southern France to fight against the remaining French forces. Germany had a partner in the fight.

As the tanks rolled into the Low Countries, Chamberlain resigned in England. It was clear that his strategy to contain Hitler was a complete failure, and he did not have the confidence of his nation to lead them in war. A new leader was needed, one who had the military experience and personal belief to see England through. Winston Churchill became prime minister. In a very short time his leadership would be put to a severe test.

19

AIMING AT ENGLAND

With most of Europe under his control, Hitler had one more major battle to fight—with Great Britain. Every other leader he had dealt with or every country he had wanted, he had simply taken by force of will and power of arms. Czech leaders had crumbled, the Norwegians had been betrayed by a leader (politician Vidkun Quisling, whose name has gone down in history as a synonym for "traitor"), the Poles had tried to resist but had failed. The tiny Low Countries had posed no threat. And France had fallen surprisingly fast.

England stood alone, untouched by Nazi forces until the summer of 1940.

Hitler at first tried his usual tactic of talking, saying only what he thought people wanted to hear, while not meaning any of it. He told Britain that it could keep its island home and most of its world-spanning empire if it simply let Germany rule the rest of Europe unopposed. While that might have worked on Chamberlain, it did not work with Churchill. The new British leader refused to bargain or even listen to Hitler. In fact, he gave several speeches outlining his refusal and starting to convince his people of the absolute need to resist Hitler at all costs. One of his most famous speeches ended with this line, "Let us therefore brace ourselves to our duties, and so bear ourselves that, if the British Empire and its Commonwealth last for a thousand years, men will still say, 'This was their finest hour.'"[70]

WINSTON CHURCHILL

Churchill was one of the towering figures of the twentieth century. Without his bulldog leadership, Great Britain might have crumbled under the Nazi bombings. Instead he rallied his nation to stay strong and united against German aggression.

Churchill was born in 1874 and spent his early life as a writer and journalist. After joining the military he fought in South Africa and later became a political leader during World War I, serving as the head of the British Navy as First Lord of the Admiralty. He faced serious failure during that war, as his decision to send troops to Gallipoli in Turkey was a disaster. He bounced back, however, and served in the government and the British cabinet between the wars. As Chamberlain led the forces of appeasement in the late 1930s, Churchill opposed the plan strongly. In 1940, Chamberlain left office, and Churchill was elected prime minister.

During the war Churchill became the symbol of a stubborn nation, refusing to give in to the Germans. His powerful speeches (see below) gave strength to his citizens, while also inspiring the world. He also proved a strong strategic leader, guiding his forces to eventual victory.

After leaving politics, he returned to his writing roots.

For his career of writing outstanding history and nonfiction, he was awarded the Nobel Prize in Literature in 1953. He had a second term as prime minister in the early 1950s too.

He passed away in 1965.

FROM A SPEECH ON JUNE 4, 1940

Even though large tracts of Europe and many old and famous States have fallen or may fall into the grip of the Gestapo and all the odious apparatus of Nazi rule, we shall not flag or fail.

We shall go on to the end, we shall fight in France,

We shall fight on the seas and oceans,

We shall fight with growing confidence and growing strength in the air,

We shall defend our Island, whatever the cost may be,

We shall fight on the beaches,

We shall fight on the landing grounds,

We shall fight in the fields and in the streets,

We shall fight in the hills;

We shall never surrender.[71]

Hitler set up a massive invasion force on the northwest coast of France, more than two hundred thousand troops. The biggest problem he faced was the twenty-one-mile wide English Channel. Soldiers, tanks, artillery, and more would have to be ferried across this thin but often stormy stretch of sea. And the British Navy was by far the strongest in the world. Also, the British air force was quite powerful and large; German forces would have to battle them as well.

Hitler and Göring decided on a softening-up strategy. They chose to attack Britain from the air, raining down bombs and bullets in an attempt to get England to surrender without an invasion. Such a massive air-only attack had never really been tried.

On August 15, 1940, the first German planes began to hit airfields and military targets inside England. Factories and other buildings were soon in ruins. British pilots poured into the sky, doing their best against the massive fleets of German planes. The battle in the sky went on for days. Wave after wave of Germany's planes headed for England, while squadrons of tiny fighters roared out to meet them.

England had, at the time, a secret weapon. They had radar.

Germany at that point did not. (Germany did, however, have carrots. A public information campaign by the British encouraged its people and soldiers to eat carrots to improve night vision. Germany started feeding its own pilots carrots to keep up. Carrots help a bit, but even rabbits can't truly see in the dark!) Having radar meant that British pilots could track the Germans coming before the Germans could see the British. That helped the British destroy many of the bombers. However, British losses were high too. In the more than three months of intense aerial fighting, more than four hundred planes were destroyed. Many bombers got through British defenses, and most of them aimed at clearly military targets. But late in August one bomber missed the mark and hit some homes and apartments. For Churchill this was crossing a line. He ordered British planes to do something that none of Germany's other enemies had been able to do since World War I—attack Germany directly.

Berlin residents were stunned when bombs dropped by British planes exploded in their beloved city.

Hitler, of course, took this as a personal and national insult, that anyone would dare to attack him and his country—even though, of course, he was doing the same thing to others. He ordered Göring to forget the military targets in Great Britain and attack cities. It was the beginning of one of the scariest times in British and European history—the Blitz.

For nearly two months, night after night, German planes rained bombs down on London. They also attacked other major cities such as Liverpool, Coventry, and Birmingham. The ancient Coventry Cathedral was destroyed by firebombs. In London thousands of civilians were killed by bombs, falling buildings, and fires. As bombers approached, searchlights lit the sky. The flashing lights were to help anti-aircraft guns target the aircraft. Sirens pierced the night, and people hurried to shelters, many of them located in London's famous subway, called the Underground. Huge thumps and falling dust frightened the people as they huddled, sometimes in the dark.

On and on the bombings went, until it seemed like London could not stand any more. But Churchill continued to rally his people, and they maintained a famous British calm amid the storm. The German people, meanwhile, were furious and wanted the bombing of their cities to stop. And the German military was losing more planes than it could afford.

What became known as the Battle of Britain finally slowed to a halt in the fall of 1940. Hitler, for the first time, had lost a military encounter. Britain's people dug out and remained resolute. Churchill knew how close his country had come to losing. In another famous speech on August 20, 1940, he said words that echo today through British and world history. His nation was in a battle for its life. He knew that without the success of his pilots in battling the German air forces, his nation and the continent—or more—might never have recovered. In the end his pilots—and his people—came through.

"The gratitude of every home in our Island, in our Empire, and indeed throughout the world, except in the abodes of the guilty, goes out to the British airmen who, undaunted by odds, unwearied in their constant challenge and mortal danger, are turning the tide of the world war by their prowess and by their devotion. Never in the field of human conflict was so much owed by so many to so few."[72]

But that "human conflict" was far from over. In fact, for many it was just beginning.

20

ATTACKING THE SOVIET UNION

After the loss in the Battle of Britain, Hitler turned his back on England. His forces still controlled most of the rest of Europe, so he left England alone to deal with later. He had even bigger plans.

His first step was to encourage and support his ally Italy as the Italians fought in North Africa. Italy, which had established colonies in North Africa in the 1930s, faced off against Great Britain, which had a huge force in Egypt, where they helped control the important Suez Canal. Hitler wanted Italy to get through the English forces and seize the canal, but he soon saw that he had to send help. He chose General Erwin Rommel, a brilliant commander of tank forces. For the next two years Rommel organized his German and Italian forces in a constant series of attacks against British troops and tanks.

The support of Italian troops came on the heels of a strengthened alliance between Hitler and Mussolini. In the fall of 1940, Hitler had also added the third leg of the Axis powers, which would form one side of World War II. In Asia the empire of Japan had, in a way, been doing what Hitler and the Nazis had been doing in Europe. In the 1930s, Japan made it clear that it wanted to expand beyond its increasingly crowded islands. It took over chunks of China and Korea and was eying expansion into the islands of the western Pacific Ocean. In 1936 it created an alliance with Germany and Italy against the Soviet Union. In 1940, Japan wanted to be clear on its place in the alliance. Hitler signed the Tripartite Pact in September 1940 with Japan and Italy. The agreement essentially gave Japan permission to do whatever it wanted in Greater Asia. It called on Japan to back

Germany's actions in Europe. More important, this was a clear signal that Germany had its eye on the United States. America saw Japan as a greater threat than Germany, not only a threat to those Pacific islands—some of which were under US control, including the then-territory of Hawaii—but also to the West Coast of America itself. The Tripartite Pact solidly connected the fates of all three Axis nations.

With that agreement in hand, however, Hitler made what turned out to be his biggest mistake while planning his largest attack yet. Though he had signed an earlier pact with Stalin promising not to attack the Soviet Union—and in fact had worked with Stalin as the Russian leader had taken eastern Poland as well as Finland and the Baltic states—Hitler had always known that that pact was a lie. It was always in his plans to take over the Communist country as well as Europe. He hated Communists almost as much as he hated Jews. Given his success with blitzkrieg in Europe, he thought he could do it again in the USSR.

He also believed that the Slavs—the ethnic group of many people east of Germany—were well down the human pecking order he had established back in *Mein Kampf*. Taking land west of Germany would be taking land from people he felt were closer to his own Aryan people. Taking land in the east fit perfectly with his aims of ridding Europe of non-Aryans.

As he contemplated his next move, Hitler tried to quietly grab Yugoslavia too, but its citizens rebelled and he bombed their capital of Belgrade. More than seventeen thousand civilians died, and with them, Yugoslavia's resistance.

In June 1941, Hitler launched Operation Barbarossa—a direct attack on the Soviet Union, with the goal of capturing its major cities. He sent more than three million soldiers into the Soviet Union's western reaches. Stalin had not believed what his own generals and staff had been telling him about Hitler's goals. The Russian Army was just not ready, and the early fighting was quick. Germany was repeating its blitzkrieg strategy with great success.

But Hitler's armies soon faced the same problem that Napoléon had faced when he too had tried to take Russia, in the early 1800s. Russia is simply enormous. To get from the eastern border of Poland to Moscow, the Soviet capital, German troops had to travel more than a thousand miles. Compare that to the distances of less than two hundred miles that they had to travel in their successful battles in the west.

RUSSIAN WINTER 1—NAPOLÉON 0

In the early 1800s Napoléon Bonaparte led France to victory after victory as he pressed his goals of a European empire. He was nearly unstoppable, conquering many countries with massive armies and lightning attacks. But as Hitler would discover more than a century later, trying to add Russia to his list of conquered countries was a step too far.

In June 1812, at the height of his power, Napoléon made the fatal error of invading Russia. One of the largest armies ever assembled poured into the flat plains of western Russia. First they faced a strong defending army. Then the heat of summer wilted them. At the gates of Moscow, France rallied, but the Russians burned most of the city rather than surrender. A counterattack forced a French retreat, and by late November the harsh Russian winter began. Temperatures plummeted, and the French troops were unprepared. Within weeks Napoléon was hurrying back to Paris, his army a shambles behind him. It was the beginning of the end of Bonaparte's career as a continent crusher.

Moving that many men and that much gear that many miles is very hard work. Plus, airplanes supporting the troops had to fly that much farther, taking more time and using more and more fuel. On a map it's a straight, relatively flat line from Poland to Moscow. But it's a long, long line, and three million men will take a long time to march or even drive it. Hitler had a plan to reach a point deep inside Russia, then split his forces in order to take the three major cities of Moscow, Stalingrad, and Leningrad at once.

By August, German forces were menacing Moscow, the capital. But then Hitler ignored his military commanders—again—because he was blinded by his hatred and mania. Instead of simply taking over the capital, he followed through on his three-for-one plan. At first it looked like it had worked. Russian troops encircled Leningrad. They also took Kiev, a major city in Ukraine, a Soviet district to the southwest. Moscow, too, was soon encircled. Stalin stayed in Moscow, but he made plans to flee if the city fell.

And then Mother Nature proved to be the winner of this conflict, no matter who had the most soldiers or dropped the most bombs. In Russia, winter is the real enemy, and Hitler had waited too long to make his moves. The fierce, freezing, snowy weather stopped his army in its tracks. Exposed and in the open, and without the equipment needed to fight or even live in such cold, the German Army was in deep trouble. For one thing, the army officers, believing that the attack would be over quickly, hadn't even brought winter clothing for most of the soldiers. The Soviet people in the encircled cities also suffered, but at least most of them could be indoors. And while the Germans struggled in the weather, Russian troops were used to it. The delay also let Stalin bring in more and more troops.

In early December, Stalin gave Hitler a taste of his own medicine. Hundreds of thousands of Soviet soldiers attacked German lines near Moscow, led by tanks and backed up by artillery. The lightning-like German attack ceased. Russian troops killed, wounded, or captured nearly a million German soldiers.

Hitler refused to let his armies give up, however, and a long, painful winter began for both German and Soviet troops.

Behind the lines of battle, however, Hitler's men were carrying out a truly evil plan. Based on Hitler's preaching about racial inferiority—and because Hitler didn't want any survivors to work against him—the German Army, SS, and Gestapo set up killing squads, known as Einsatzgruppen. The squads were tasked with following the advancing German armies as they marched east, finding Russian officials, and killing them. The squads were also to kill Slavs and Jews and anyone that Hitler found offensive. Small groups of soldiers shot tens of thousands of people. It was simple murder on a mass, organized scale. Sadly, they kept careful records that show, for example, that 33,771 men, women, and children were shot and killed in one small area in Ukraine in early September 1941. Himmler decided that shooting was not fast enough and that it was hard on his men, so he looked into using sealed trucks filled with poison gas. That idea spread to the concentration camps, and by late in 1941, Nazi totals showed that more than 630,000 people had been killed.

What was happening? How could people do this to other people? Hitler and his cronies believed that those being executed were not really people. A Nazi leader in Ukraine put it plainly: "We are a master race, which must remember that the lowliest German worker is racially and biologically a thousand times more valuable than the population here."[73]

Russian soldiers who had been captured fared little better. Though throughout modern history, nations have treated their prisoners of war humanely most of the time, here the Nazis once again ignored history and morality. More than three million Russian prisoner-soldiers would die in the course of the war, most as a result of hunger, cold, or overwork.

Here was another instance when people—his generals and other top military leaders—could have spoken up against Hitler. They knew that all this killing was wrong. It was against the military code with which they had been raised, some before World War I even. Could they have tried to stop it? They were afraid of what might happen, of course. They were also afraid of losing their important jobs. Did they agree with Hitler's aims? Some did, to a degree, but most did not. Hitler succeeded in large part because people—even those closest to him and with the best chance of doing something to stop him—refused to take action against him.

THOUGH HE WAS making good on his deadly promises to kill Jews, Slavs, Communists, and others, Hitler was no longer winning on the battlefield. He had overextended his forces, ignored his military leaders, and believed only in his own vision. His air force had been hammered by Britain. His army was freezing to death in Russia. And more bad news was coming, though he didn't see it that way at the time.

On December 7, 1941, Japanese airplanes flying off aircraft carriers attacked the US Navy at Pearl Harbor, Hawaii. The totally unexpected attack left the US Pacific Fleet in ruins. More than two thousand soldiers, sailors, and civilians were killed. Eighteen ships were destroyed or sunk, including the USS *Arizona* on which more than 1,100 service members died. The next day the US declared war on Japan.

Hitler, supporting his Japanese ally through the Tripartite

Pact and knowing that his action would draw the United States into the European fight for the first time, beat the United States to the punch and declared his own war on America on December 11. America followed with its own declaration against Germany.

Hitler's European war had now truly become World War II.

21

THE FINAL SOLUTION

As his armies ranged throughout the east and west of Germany, Hitler saw his plans for Lebensraum being realized—if he could hold on to the lands. However, the plan that was more important to him could now take even more terrible effect. After speaking out against the Jews for more than a dozen years, after passing law after law that made German Jewish lives miserable, after carrying his war against the Jews into Poland, Austria, Czechoslovakia, and the Soviet Union . . . even after all that, he was not done. He ordered Reinhard Heydrich, a key Nazi aide, to plan the "Final Solution" to the Jewish problem. After a constant series of awful blows against Jews, Hitler, it appeared, was ready to go all the way. He ordered a genocide of Jewish people in Europe.

Believe it or not, the Nazis actually held a conference to talk about how they would do this. In January 1942, a group of top Nazi officials from various branches of the military and the government—but not Hitler himself—gathered in a Berlin building for a meeting that took its fateful name from the street where the building was located. The Wannsee Conference was a planning meeting for mass murder.

They were fulfilling the clear wishes of the führer. Among the many statements Hitler made on the topic was this from a 1942 speech: "We realize that this war can only end either in the wiping out of the Germanic nations, or by the disappearance of Jewry from Europe."[74]

The officials at the Wannsee Conference discussed some of the ways they had killed people already, including mass shootings, individual shootings, poisonings, and the use of gas. They talked about using sealed trucks and about building gas chambers. They looked at the places where they could construct the gas chambers, noting the concentration camps they had already set up in Germany and in Poland, among other locations.

Heydrich addressed the other men, saying that it was their job to take on "the responsibility for working out the final solution of the Jewish problem regardless of geographical boundaries."[75] That meant that wherever the German army roamed, Jews would die.

The conference wrapped up with the members getting their orders. Some arranged trains for the prisoners, while others looked to the building of more and more camps. Still others were charged with setting up groups of soldiers and other people to find Jews. Even medical experts were consulted on the best methods for mass killing.

Places in Poland became the main death sites. At six of the sites tens of thousands of people were killed after being treated as little more than two-legged cattle. At one camp the people were herded, naked, into sealed rooms, and truck exhaust was piped in. The deadly fumes killed by suffocating. Some rooms were so packed with people that the dead could not even fall over. Soon the camp at Auschwitz was using a gas called Zyklon B that did the job faster than exhaust fumes.

In June two Czech soldiers who had seen the awful things that the Heydrich-led Nazis were doing tried to stop things. They attacked Heydrich with grenades and a machine gun as he rode in a car near Prague. Heydrich died soon after of his wounds.

The Nazi revenge for this assassination was terrible. Thousands of Czechs—whether Jews or not—were killed in reprisal. An entire village was burned down and every male killed. And the killings in the camps continued too, now led by the possibly even more awful Heinrich Himmler.

At camp after camp a terrible ritual happened. Men, women, and children were marched out of packed, stinking railroad cars that had rolled for days from east and west. If the men or women were seen as healthy enough to be put to work in factories making things for the German soldiers, they were pulled aside. Everyone else was marched away to die. Those who were going to be killed were first stripped of clothing. Often the women had their heads shaved. They were shoved into the gas chambers. And after they died, soldiers searched for gold fillings in their teeth.

Those "lucky" enough to work fared little better. They worked long hours in very cold or very hot places and were given little food or water. Many died from overwork. Others died from illnesses they contracted because of the terrible conditions.

Jews arrived at the camps from all over Europe. Shamefully, they were turned in by their countrymen in France. They were captured in the Netherlands, in Belgium, and in Denmark. They were dragged from their homes in Poland and Austria. And they came from the east after German troops poured through the far eastern part of the Soviet Union. The number of deaths grew and grew . . . and it was only 1942.

Additionally, when German soldiers found "Aryans" among the people they were capturing—blond, blue-eyed children of any background—the children were sent back to Germany to be raised there as Nazis. In this way thousands of children were kidnapped.

There was more. At several camps, medical experiments were done on Jewish and other victims. Horrible things were done to "learn" more about humans and their ability to withstand pain or to survive various wounds or gassings.

Among the many, many terrible and sad stories to come out of the Holocaust was that of a young Jewish girl. Anne Frank and her family left Germany in 1933 as the Nazis power grew. They moved to Amsterdam, only to have the Nazis arrive there, too, in 1940. For the next four years the Frank family hid with friends, eventually finding room in a small attic, from which Anne could only peer through a tiny window as her world collapsed. Throughout much of her time there, Anne kept a diary about her experiences. The Franks were finally found and sent to camps in 1944, where Anne died.

Anne's father, Otto, survived the camps, and in 1947 arranged to have his daughter's words published. The diary of Anne Frank has become one of the most-loved and most-read books in the world, telling the personal and poignant story of a young person in the midst of one of the world's greatest horrors. Her humanity and maturity shine through in this remarkable work.

How could people do this to other people? How could soldiers believe so blindly in their leader that they would spend days doing nothing but shooting people in the head as those people knelt over open graves?

"Don't you see," one soldier said much later. "We SS men were not supposed to think about these things. It never even occurred to us. We were trained to obey orders, without even thinking, [so] that the thought of disobeying an order would simply never have occurred to anybody. Somebody else would have done it just as well if I hadn't."[76]

Himmler was clear on that point too, at one time saying that SS men who failed in their duty would "die without mercy."[77] Himmler spoke of the Jewish people as "a bacterium" that he had to "cauterize."[78] That means he thought of them as a germ to be burned.

22

HITLER STARTS LOSING

As 1942 began, Germany was fighting a war on three fronts. In the west it was facing little resistance from French and English forces. In the south English troops were fighting back in Greece against Italian and German forces. In the east Germany's assault on the Soviet Union was going badly. The United States would not play a major role in Europe at first, focusing most of its attention on Japan and the battle in the Pacific. However, the United States increased its supplies to England and the other Allies.

Hitler, struggling with bad health brought on by the stress of the war, was also struggling to control the many branches of his army. He continued to maintain total control even as events got more and more complicated. He also refused to admit defeat or retreat; generals who suggested either were immediately replaced. Meanwhile, his relationship with Eva Braun continued in secret. She was not allowed to be part of any of his decisions or meetings. She spent most of her time at Berchtesgaden, Hitler's retreat in the German Alps. When she was in Berlin, she was never seen with Hitler. The only times she was near him came when she was working for the Nazi Party photographer. Only his closest aides knew of their relationship. To these aides Hitler repeatedly said that he would never marry, since he had to save himself for Germany and could not be distracted by a family. Over time Braun came to accept this role, and she would remain devoted to him to the end.

After many successes in North Africa, Erwin Rommel finally was defeated for good in a massive tank battle at El Alamein in

Egypt. Nazi control of North Africa went with him, as did any chance they would have had at securing the Suez Canal.

More bad news came from the east. Hitler had ordered his cold, hungry troops to stage a massive attack at the large Soviet city of Stalingrad. But by late 1942 his attack had turned into a defeat. The defenders of Stalingrad inspired all of Russia by refusing to give up. In fact, they fought back so fiercely that they ended up surrounding a massive German army. Hitler tried to send help by plane, but it was never enough.

The winter weather crushed the trapped Germans. Thousands died from frostbite or hunger. Yet Hitler just kept changing generals. In one message he wrote, "Surrender out of the question. Troops will resist to the end."[79] These were not the words of a competent military commander. They were the words of someone who more and more people inside Germany—and certainly those outside—were coming to see as a madman. Finally, on February 2, 1943, after months of desperation, German forces surrendered. Because Russian troops had been so badly treated, surrendering to the Russians did not improve things that much for the German soldiers, and tens of thousands of them died as prisoners.

Yet back in Germany, Goebbels, at Hitler's orders, simply told the German people that they were not trying hard enough. The Nazis called for "total war," the use of all people—men and women—to do everything they could to defeat the enemy. Even as their soldiers died in Russia, the Germans were told that the way to victory was "the total and radical extermination and elimination of Jewry."[80]

In March 1943, Hitler was nearly exterminated himself—again. An assassination plot led by some German generals arranged for a bomb to be planted on a plane Hitler was flying on. The bomb was set to go off in flight. But the plane landed safely, and later the plotters learned that the bomb had malfunctioned. Another plot failed a few days later when Hitler unexpectedly left the place where the assassin was supposed to strike.

In July, after suffering numerous military losses, Mussolini was forced to give up his position as head of Italy. Hitler was shocked by this, and these actions prevented Italy from continuing as his ally.

In late July, the city of Hamburg in Germany was nearly destroyed by a massive bombing attack by Allied forces.

Also that month, Germany suffered another massive loss in the Soviet Union. Nazi troops assaulted the city of Kursk on the western Soviet border. The battle raged for a month and included one of the largest tank battles ever fought, but in the end Russian troops won. Hitler's dream of taking over the Soviet Union died with the defeat.

Hitler did have one small moment of triumph. He approved a secret mission to "rescue" Mussolini from a mountainside building where he was being held prisoner by Italian authorities. In a raid that would be considered a daring triumph if not for the madman was doing the raiding, a team led by Captain Otto Skorzeny landed gliders on the high, flat plateau. They surprised the few guards and got Mussolini out in a small plane. (Hitler expected Mussolini to charge back in and take command of Italy, and while Mussolini did so briefly, he was a shell of his former imposing self.)

Through all of Hitler's losses, he remained adamant. He would not negotiate. He would not talk to his enemies. He would demand more and more of his armies and his people, and he would not stop until he had won . . . or until he was dead.

And throughout it all, in the camps in eastern Germany and in the lands farther east, the gas chambers kept filling up and the fires kept burning. In fact, in early 1944, Himmler reported news to a gathering of party officials, proudly stating that "the Jewish question has been solved. Six million have been killed."[81]

More would follow.

⤝ 23 ⤞

D-DAY

While Hitler ranted at his generals, and his men killed on an unimaginable scale, a plan was forming that would prove to be his final undoing.

American, English, French, and other Allied forces were planning a massive invasion of Europe from the west that they hoped would finally turn the tide against Germany. In the east the Soviet Union, now firmly a part of the Allies (though Stalin, of course, had other plans), was clearly winning its fight with Hitler. That left the west as the next battleground.

To get enough troops into France—the best place from which to start an invasion—the Allies would have to mount the largest amphibious landing ever. That meant they would have to carry millions of men and an incredible amount of gear across the English Channel. And they had to do it without getting all those ships sunk or those men killed before they could find a safe place on land. Hitler knew this, of course, and had built huge fortifications along the northwestern French coast. He also had tank divisions waiting inside the countryside to attack any landing party.

"If we succeed in throwing back the invasion," Hitler said in early 1944, "such an attempt [the invasion] cannot and will not be repeated. It will mean our reserves will be set free to use in Italy and the East."[82]

So because the Allies knew that Hitler knew this, they pulled off one of the greatest fakes of all time. For months they let Hitler hear about their plans to attack Calais, the point in France that is closest to England—the shortest trip across the Channel. The Allies did this by sending messages to Germany through spies that they had captured and turned. That is, they forced German spies to report only news that the Allies provided. They also created enormous armies of soldiers that existed only on paper, built wooden airplanes so that Hitler's spy flights would spot them, and created a massive network of misdirection. It was almost like a magic trick.

And it worked.

By summer the Allied forces were finally ready to spring their trap. All that was needed was good weather and a few final misdirections. In early June, news from England reached Hitler that the landing was coming at Calais soon. The Allied landing, code-named D-Day, was set for June 4, but weather prevented the actual landing from taking place until June 6. That morning Allied ships started sending thundering curtains of artillery toward beaches in Normandy, a region in France more than fifty miles southwest of Calais. The artillery was followed by an enormous flotilla of ships pouring across the Channel. At the moment when the shells began to land, Hitler was asleep, and no one wanted to wake him for hours. Frozen by the lack of orders, German tanks sat idle.

The Allies were met with resistance, and thousands of men died in the surf without ever reaching European soil. But their fellow soldiers fought on, and in many places pushed through the German lines guarding the beaches.

Even after Hitler was finally awoken and given the news several hours after the attack had begun, he believed it to be a false attack. He was convinced that the real invasion was still to come at Calais. And since he had established a world in which no one could question him, no one really did. Tanks were sent to Calais to meet a threat that was not there. Within days the Allies had broken out from the beaches and were streaming across France.

D-DAY AND BEYOND

The Allied invasion of Europe on June 6, 1944—known as D-Day—was the largest such landing in world history. Millions of troops and thousands of ships, planes, and tanks took part. Planned in complete secrecy, the D-Day landings proved successful and led to the end of World War II.

The basic plan was for Allied forces to attack several points on the Normandy coast. Beaches with code names such as Juno, Sword, and Omaha became the sites of fierce fighting and amazing courage. Soldiers stormed the beach through machine-gun fire, while sailors returned again and again with landing craft, even as artillery blasted at them.

After establishing beachheads at many of the landing sites, the Allied soldiers quickly moved inland to make room for more soldiers and the tons of supplies arriving behind them. The rapid rush of Allied forces into northern France turned the tide of the war. The foothold gained by D-Day, at the cost of more than ten thousand men killed and thousands more wounded, became the starting point for the defeat of Hitler's Germany.

Hitler's domination of the army and his total personal control was proving to be his undoing. He trusted almost none of his generals, but the few he did trust were not in a position to stop him or change his mind. Over and over they simply did what they were ordered to do, even when they, as experts, knew it was wrong. Hitler had always been unbalanced, but they saw him drifting further and further into paranoia as the losses mounted.

In fact, he continued to ignore the generals who said that the Allies were dominating them and that a retreat to regroup was vital. Instead Hitler ordered new and deadly attacks with the new V1 rockets. He ordered them fired at London, and more than two hundred hit their targets. It was Hitler's plan to make England surrender or face more rocket attacks. But as they had during the Blitz, England "kept calm and carried on."

In July 1944 some of the German generals finally tried to do something about Hitler. A few of them helped put together a plot to kill the führer so that Germany could salvage something and end the war. They planted a bomb in a meeting room, but just moments before it was set to go off, Hitler got up and left. Once again he was lucky. The bomb destroyed much of the room. Hitler was dazed and bruised but alive. He bragged about the burns on his clothing. Later he complained of a hearing loss that turned out to be a ruptured eardrum, and he probably suffered a serious concussion. More important, the close call again played into his belief that he was destined to remain alive for victory, that nothing could stop him. The men who had started the plot were caught and killed. More than five thousand others suspected of helping or supporting the plan were also killed. Many were community or political leaders who would have been needed to run the country after Hitler. Others were military leaders. Hitler supposedly watched film of some of the hangings.

One of the generals, a man named Tresckow, who committed suicide rather than face execution, wrote before he died, "Everybody will now turn upon us and cover us with abuse. But my conviction remains unshaken—we have done the right thing. Hitler is not only the archenemy of Germany—he is the archenemy of the world."[83]

About a month after that ill-timed bomb, Allied forces rolled into Paris, finally liberating that famous city from Nazi rule. France was free, and soon the Low Countries were too, along with Denmark and Norway, as the German army rolled backward toward its homeland. It looked like the war was ending, but then Germany stopped and made one more push back toward the west. In the thick forests of Belgium, German troops made a stand, and the Battle of the Bulge began.

24

ONE LAST BATTLE

Hitler was very ill. The assassination attempt had weakened him. He was already taking dozens of pills and getting injections of various things that his many doctors thought he needed. He was sticking to his vegetarian diet but not eating very much. He was also, his doctors discovered, taking pills that he thought would help but that were actually very bad for him. Tests showed that his heart was getting weaker too. The stress of the war was killing him.

But he was still in charge. As he listened to his generals recount the massive losses, especially in the west as Allied forces continued to advance, he suddenly had an idea. He saw a way to try to strike back, even though most of the previous year the German forces had been on the defensive. He came up with a plan to use men led by the courageous commando Otto Skorzeny to pretend to be American troops. They would be put into the forests of Belgium, in an area known as the Ardennes. Their mission would be to confuse and surprise advancing American units and set them up for attack by German tanks.

By mid-December all the plans were in place and Hitler sprang the trap, which he called Autumn Fog. More than 250,000 German soldiers poured into the area. Tanks followed, and Skorzeny's men sowed confusion. Soon Americans were not sure who they were aiming at—Germans or fellow Americans. On a map the lines showing the German break through the Allied positions gave the event its famous name, the Battle of the Bulge. The American troops were outnumbered at first. Hitler knew that bad weather was typical for this time of year, so the American air support could not fly overhead and provide cover for the advancing forces. The tank attack caught the Americans by surprise. For a couple of weeks toward the end of 1944, it looked as if Germany might have one more blitzkrieg to brag about. It was Hitler's last stand.

But it didn't last. American troops held on bravely until help arrived. American and Allied airplanes were able to attack German positions when the weather cleared. The Battle of the Bulge wound down by early January.

In Berlin even the loyal Hermann Göring, whom Hitler had picked to take over Germany should the führer die, was talking about negotiating an end to the war. Hitler erupted, screaming at his number two, "I forbid you to take any step in this matter. If you go against my orders, I will have you shot."[84]

Hitler's ability to reason was clearly going. General Heinz Guderian, appointed to lead the army after the failed assassination plot, later wrote, "He believed no one anymore. It had been difficult enough dealing with him. It now became a torture that grew steadily worse from month to month. He frequently lost all self-control and his language grew increasingly violent."[85]

Allied forces headed toward Berlin. From the east the Soviet

Red Army did the same. As they did, they began to reveal, in early 1945, the concentration camps. For the first time the wider world saw the horrors of Hitler's evil. Images of the haggard, starving prisoners were seen worldwide. The Soviets found evidence of the gas chambers and the killing rooms. They discovered piles of clothing, rooms of gold teeth, and bodies buried everywhere. Reporters who visited struggled to come up with words to describe something that they, and the world, would never forget.

American and British troops liberated other camps. General Dwight Eisenhower, supreme commander of the Allies, visited one and said, "I never dreamed that such cruelty, bestiality, and savagery could really exist in this world!"[86]

(It should be pointed out that the Soviets were in some ways not much better than the Nazis. They often killed civilians in the towns they captured, and raping women was common. People in western Russia, in Poland, and in eastern Germany so feared the Russians that they sometimes killed themselves rather than be forced to live as Soviet citizens. What the Red Army was doing was starting the Soviet rule of these captured territories. This totalitarian conquest was the beginning of the Cold War between East and West, which would go on until the early 1990s. American and British forces, by contrast, were greeted with flowers, parades, and joy.)

But on the ground now, the race was one to rid the world of Hitler and the Nazis. It was just a matter of who would get there first.

Hitler knew they were coming, and by February 1945 he had moved into a series of underground bunkers beneath Berlin. They were complete with communications gear; gas generators to supply air, heat, and light; and several rooms for sleeping, eating, and holding meetings. His inner circle of advisers was with him, including several visiting doctors, who continued to fill him with pills. Eva Braun came to live with him in the bunker, in a separate pair of rooms set aside for the couple. She feared that the end was coming, but she chose to make the final stand with Hitler.

By this time perhaps Hitler's mind was gone. One of his regular visitors was an architect named Paul Giesler. Together he and Hitler toyed with a large wooden model of Linz, Austria—Hitler's former home. They were planning how they would rebuild it even better and more beautifully. They even put up lights so people could see how the city of the future would look at different times of the day. Meanwhile, above Hitler's head Berlin itself was being destroyed, day by day, by endless Allied bombing.

Hitler ordered that every man left in Germany join the Volkssturm, the People's Army. He made teenagers and old men join. He emptied the schools and even made women who could carry weapons take to the streets. The Hitler Youth became a teenage army. Thousands died defending a land they probably barely recognized because it was so shattered by years of war and destruction.

As the news got worse and worse, Hitler tried one final desperate act. He ordered his retreating armies to destroy what was left of Germany. He told them to destroy bridges, dams, buildings, museums, everything. Shockingly—though at this point, it's hard to be shocked by anything Hitler did—he blamed all of his losses on his own people. In giving the order to destroy the country, he basically said he didn't care one way or the other about them. "This nation will have proved to be the weaker one and the future will belong solely to the stronger eastern nation [the Soviet Union]. Besides, those who will remain after the battle are only the inferior ones, for the good ones have all been killed."[87]

Fortunately, few commanders followed this order, and some of the leaders still aboveground didn't even pass these orders on. Here, finally, Hitler's followers rebelled, and very little of the damage he had called for was inflicted.

On April 20, 1945, Adolf Hitler turned fifty-six. It was his last birthday.

25

THE DEATH OF HITLER

A few days before his birthday, Hitler had gotten some good news. President Roosevelt had died on April 12. Harry Truman took over as US president. Hitler thought there was a chance that Truman would not be quite the powerful enemy that FDR had been. He was wrong, so his joy was very short-lived.

Those remaining belowground with Hitler celebrated his birthday with a small party. Göring was there, as was Goebbels.

Some of the top remaining military men were there. Eva was there, of course.

Hitler would not leave. He did not want to be captured by the Russians any more than his countrymen to the east wanted such a fate. But he knew the end was near, finally. He let most of the staff and others escape while they could. Meanwhile, radio broadcasts let remaining Germans know that their führer was staying in Berlin.

On April 22, Hitler had a final rant. He screamed and yelled and blamed everyone else for the failure of the war. Even though his aides had seen such outbursts before, this was a memorable one. Göring, Himmler, and others took this as their cue to leave. Göring wrote to Hitler the next day, asking if he could take over as Germany's leader after Hitler. Himmler even took it on himself to contact Allied leaders to try to work out a surrender. But no one was going to negotiate with the leader of the SS after seeing what his camps had done.

After reading Göring's telegram and then hearing of Himmler's failed attempts to surrender, Hitler went ballistic again. All of his closest aides and longtime followers had finally deserted him.

News soon reached the bunker of the death of Mussolini. The former Italian leader had been shot by a firing squad to answer for his many crimes against Italy. A mob later dragged his body through the streets and hung it upside down from the girders of a gas station after kicking it and beating it with sticks. Hitler was shocked by the way his former ally had died.

Early in the morning of April 29, Hitler and Eva Braun were married. Hitler had for years said that he could not marry because his sole focus had to be on Germany. As he faced the end, however, he decided this was the time.

In the afternoon Hitler gave a cyanide pill to his beloved German shepherd dog, Blondi. This was to test the pills, which Hitler didn't believe would really work. The pills worked. Hitler's dog died. Later that day Hitler dictated a long final will and testament, once again laying blame on others and making his last angry racist claims against the Jews.

On April 30, Hitler said good-bye to the few people remaining in the underground bunker. He and Eva went into their bedroom and closed the door.

Hitler then gave a cyanide pill to Eva Braun, who took it

and died. Like Hitler, she did not want to be left at the hands of the oncoming Russian forces. Hitler took a pill himself as well. Then, to be sure of his fate, he did what millions of people around the world probably had wished they could have done—and what millions wished he had done much earlier: Hitler shot himself in the head.

After hearing the shot, an aide entered the room and found the couple's dead bodies. Following instructions Hitler had left, the two bodies were burned so that they could not be paraded as Mussolini's had.

Hitler's death was announced to Germany and the world on May 1.

On May 7, Germany officially surrendered to the Allies.

EPILOGUE: AFTER HITLER

In the days and weeks following Hitler's death, Germany and the world reeled from the ongoing revelations about the death camps. What has come to be known as the Holocaust was discovered day by day as the camps were liberated and the remaining captives—starved, skeleton-like, and desperate—were let out. They clamored for food and water and clung to their rescuers. Or else they simply continued staring in disbelief at all that they had witnessed.

Investigations by the Allies uncovered the thousands and thousands of mass graves in and around the camps. The Allies also found the terrible machinery of death—ovens, cremation chambers, sealed gas rooms, surgery rooms where medical experiments had been carried out, and much more. Hitler's nightmarish vision for the destruction of the Jewish people in Europe had come close to full reality. More than six million Jews died in Germany, Poland, the Soviet Union, Austria, and throughout the rest of Europe. Millions of others who did not meet the Nazis' racial standards also died—Gypsies (now known as Rom), disabled people, orphans, Communists, and even Catholics. The scale of mass death was shocking, and in terms of sheer numbers, only Stalin's purges in the Soviet Union before and after the war could match it.

So who was held responsible for all this death? Hitler, of course, escaped punishment by killing himself. Many of his top aides chose that way out too, including Göring, Himmler, and Goebbels, who killed his six children with help from his wife, before killing her and then himself. Trials were held in Nuremberg starting in 1945 and thousands of Nazi officials and military leaders were found guilty of war crimes. Some were executed by hanging; others were given long prison sentences. Some joined the growing ranks of Nazi suicides.

The effect of the Holocaust on the Jewish people will never end. Millions of Jewish families, many now scattered around the world or living in the new state of Israel, founded in 1948, maintain the memories and connections to that terrible time. They wonder about the relatives they never met, the branches of their families that disappeared. They tell the story of the Holocaust, generation after generation, in books, films, recordings, and more. Their enduring cry is simply, "Never forget."

AS WORLD WAR II ended, another war began—the Cold War. The Soviet Union took advantage of the chaos in Europe to establish its own expanded empire on its western flank, taking over Poland, Hungary, Yugoslavia, the Baltic states, and the eastern part of Germany. Within the new East Germany was Berlin, which itself was divided by the Allies into four parts after the war. The American, British, and French sectors were open, while the Soviet sector was soon a closed, guarded place. By the late 1950s the entire city of Berlin was encircled by the Soviet-controlled East Germany—and West Berlin, as the Allied sectors came to be known, was an island of the West behind the Iron Curtain of the East.

But Hitler didn't really cause that; Stalin and the Soviet leaders who followed him were responsible. For his part Hitler left behind a shattered Germany, with citizens full of remorse for what they had done, and full of guilt for their often-silent part in the horrors of the Holocaust. While the details of the camps might not have been widely known—or not widely believed—there was no doubt at all that the German people had accepted Hitler's and the Nazis' treatment of Jews and other non-Aryans. Their acceptance had let Hitler believe he could continue. And he had continued, with terrifying results.

SEVEN DECADES LATER, Germany is the most prosperous nation in Europe and once again a world leader. The shadows of its Nazi past fade more and more each year. But sometimes the past rises up to be remembered. In 2015 refugees from Syria and other embattled Middle Eastern nations began pouring into Europe.

In a striking change from how the nation had treated outsiders in the 1930s, Germany welcomed thousands of Syrian and other refugees. Some in the country objected, however, and their strident anti-outsider cries could have been heard in the streets of Munich in 1930.

In 2016, Hitler's book *Mein Kampf* was published in Germany for the first time since the war. The book had been banned since then. The new edition, however, was packed with thousands of notes from scholars and historians pointing out Hitler's many false claims and mistakes. The book sold out in its first week in stores. Let's hope it was bought by people who wanted to read the footnotes.

AUTHOR'S NOTE

This was a hard book to write. Hitler and the Nazis did many, many really awful and horrible things. I didn't want to look at some of the pictures or watch some of the videos, but I did. You should too. They are in some ways more powerful than words we put on these pages. I also don't want this book to honor Hitler in any way. He was a monster, a madman who grabbed power and created evil. Believe it or not, there are people alive today, walking among us, who think he was some sort of hero. Don't listen to those people. This guy was sick. I'm supposed to be objective and just tell the story, tell the facts, so you can understand what happened. But in telling some stories, that's just not enough. I'm sorry you had to read some of the things in this book, but it's worth experiencing some discomfort in order to understand how evil can come to be in this world. Those feelings of discomfort are nothing compared to what tens of millions of people experienced because of Hitler and his followers. It's up to us now, to make sure no one like him ever gets such a chance again.

I worked with several key sources in writing this account of Adolf Hitler. Some are aimed at younger readers, while others are for a general audience or for scholars. This is a partial listing of what I relied on for research.

John Toland, *Adolf Hitler* (New York: Random House, 1976).

Paul Ham, *Young Hitler* (London: Endeavour Press, 2014).

Sean Stewart Price, *Adolf Hitler: A Wicked History* (New York: Franklin Watts, 2009).

Liz Gogerly, *Adolf Hitler: From Failed Artist to Fascist Dictator* (New York: Franklin Watts, 2002).

William Shirer, *Berlin Diary: Journal of a Foreign Correspondent, 1934–41* (Baltimore: Johns Hopkins University Press, 2002).

Joachim Fest, *Hitler* (New York: Harcourt, 1973).

The History Place (historyplace.com)

BBC.com

History.com

TIME LINE

1889	Adolf Hitler is born in Austria.
1903	Hitler's father dies.
1907	Hitler fails an art exam.
	Hitler's mother dies.
1908	Hitler moves to Vienna, Austria.
	Hitler fails an art exam for the second time.
1913	Hitler moves to Munich, Germany.
1914	World War I begins.
1918	World War I ends with German defeat.
1919	The Treaty of Versailles is signed.
	Hitler joins the German Workers' Party.
1920	The Nazi Party forms.
1921	Hitler is named leader of the Nazi Party.
1923	The Beer Hall Putsch occurs.
	Hitler is sentenced to prison.
1925	*Mein Kampf* is published.
1930	The Nazi Party becomes the second-largest political party in Germany.

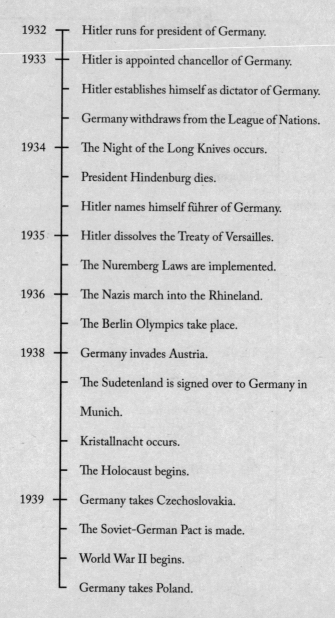

1932 — Hitler runs for president of Germany.

1933 — Hitler is appointed chancellor of Germany.

— Hitler establishes himself as dictator of Germany.

— Germany withdraws from the League of Nations.

1934 — The Night of the Long Knives occurs.

— President Hindenburg dies.

— Hitler names himself führer of Germany.

1935 — Hitler dissolves the Treaty of Versailles.

— The Nuremberg Laws are implemented.

1936 — The Nazis march into the Rhineland.

— The Berlin Olympics take place.

1938 — Germany invades Austria.

— The Sudetenland is signed over to Germany in Munich.

— Kristallnacht occurs.

— The Holocaust begins.

1939 — Germany takes Czechoslovakia.

— The Soviet-German Pact is made.

— World War II begins.

— Germany takes Poland.

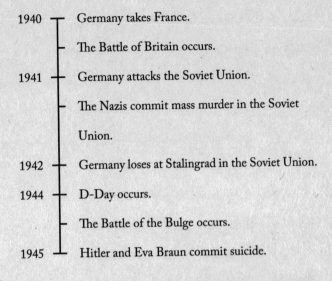

1940 — Germany takes France.

— The Battle of Britain occurs.

1941 — Germany attacks the Soviet Union.

— The Nazis commit mass murder in the Soviet

Union.

1942 — Germany loses at Stalingrad in the Soviet Union.

1944 — D-Day occurs.

— The Battle of the Bulge occurs.

1945 — Hitler and Eva Braun commit suicide.

NOTES

1. John Toland. *Adolf Hitler* (New York: Random House, 1976). Kindle edition, chapter 1.

2. Toland, *Adolf Hitler*, chapter 1.

3. Toland, *Adolf Hitler*, chapter 1.

4. Paul Ham, *Young Hitler* (London: Endeavour Press, 2014). Kindle edition, chapter 2.

5. Toland, *Adolf Hitler*, chapter 1.

6. Ham, *Young Hitler,* chapter 2.

7. Ham, *Young Hitler,* chapter 2.

8. Toland, *Adolf Hitler*, chapter 1, section 2.

9. Ham, *Young Hitler,* chapter 2.

10. Toland, *Adolf Hitler*, chapter 1, section 2.

11. Ham, *Young Hitler,* chapter 3.

12. Ham, *Young Hitler,* chapter 3.

13. Toland, *Adolf Hitler*, chapter 3.

14. Ham, *Young Hitler,* chapter 2.

15. Toland, *Adolf Hitler*, chapter 2.

16. Toland, *Adolf Hitler*, chapter 3.

17. Liz Gogerly, *Adolf Hitler: From Failed Artist to Fascist Dictator* (New York: Franklin Watts, 2002), 19.

18. Toland, *Adolf Hitler*, chapter 3, section 2.

19. Toland, *Adolf Hitler*, chapter 3, section 2.

20. Toland, *Adolf Hitler*, chapter 3, section 2.

21. Ham, *Young Hitler,* chapter 4.

22. Ham, *Young Hitler,* chapter 4.

23. Toland, *Adolf Hitler*, chapter 5.

24. Toland, *Adolf Hitler*, chapter 5.

25. Toland, *Adolf Hitler*, chapter 5.

26. Ham, *Young Hitler,* chapter 4.

27. Ham, *Young Hitler,* chapter 3, section 3.

28. Toland, *Adolf Hitler*, chapter 3, section 3.

29. Ham, *Young Hitler,* chapter 6.

30. hitler.org/writings/Mein_Kampf/mkv1ch09.html.

31. Toland, *Adolf Hitler*, chapter 3.

32. Toland, *Adolf Hitler*, chapter 4.

33. Toland, *Adolf Hitler*, chapter 4.

34. Toland, *Adolf Hitler*, chapter 4.

35. Toland, *Adolf Hitler*, chapter 4.

36. Toland, *Adolf Hitler*, chapter 4, section 4.

37. Toland, *Adolf Hitler*, chapter 5, section 3.

38. Joachim Fest, *Hitler* (New York: Harcourt, 1973), 144.

39. Toland, *Adolf Hitler*, chapter 5.

40. Ham, *Young Hitler,* chapter 4.

41. Toland, *Adolf Hitler*, chapter 6.

42. William Shirer, *Berlin Diary: Journal of a Foreign Correspondent, 1934–41* (Baltimore: Johns Hopkins University Press, 2002), 75.

43. Ham, *Young Hitler,* chapter 7.

44. Toland, *Adolf Hitler*, chapter 10.

45. Toland, *Adolf Hitler*, chapter 10.

46. Fest, *Hitler*, 567.

47. Toland, *Adolf Hitler*, chapter 11.

48. Toland, *Adolf Hitler*, chapter 11, section 2.

49. Toland, *Adolf Hitler*, chapter 11, section 4.

50. Toland, *Adolf Hitler*, chapter 11, section 4.

51. Toland, *Adolf Hitler*, chapter 11, section 3.

52. Toland, *Adolf Hitler*, chapter 11, section 3.

53. Shirer, *Berlin Diary*, 18.

54. Ian Kershaw, *To Hell and Back* (New York: Viking, 2015). Kindle edition, chapter 6.

55. Shirer, *Berlin Diary*, 286.

56. pbs.org/wgbh/amex/goebbels/peopleevents/e_olympics.html. Quoting Jeremiah Mahoney.

57. Toland, *Adolf Hitler*, chapter 18, section 3.

58. Fest, *Hitler*, 567.

59. Holocaust Encyclopedia Online, "Kristallnacht," ushmm.org/information /exhibitions/online-exhibitions/special-focus/kristallnacht.

60. Toland, *Adolf Hitler*, chapter 18.

61. Toland, *Adolf Hitler*, chapter 18, section 2.

62. Toland, *Adolf Hitler*, chapter 19.

63. Toland, *Adolf Hitler*, chapter 19.

64. Toland, *Adolf Hitler*, chapter 19, section 1.

65. Toland, *Adolf Hitler*, chapter 20, section 3.

66. Toland, *Adolf Hitler*, chapter 21.

67. Toland, *Adolf Hitler*, chapter 21.

68. Shirer, *Berlin Diary*, 742.

69. Martin Winstone, *Dark Heart of Hitler's Europe: Nazi Rule in Poland under the General Government* (London: I.B. Tauris, 2015), 96.

70. The Churchill Centre, "Speeches, June 18, 1940," winstonchurchill.org/resources /speeches.

71. The Churchill Centre, "Speeches, June 4, 1940," winstonchurchill.org/resources /speeches.

72. The Churchill Centre, "Speeches, August 15, 1940," winstonchurchill.org/resources /speeches.

73. Marvin Perry, *World War II in Europe: A Concise History* (Boston: Wadsworth, 2013), 103.

74. Toland, *Adolf Hitler*, chapter 25, section 1.

75. Toland, *Adolf Hitler*, chapter 19, section 3.

76. Toland, *Adolf Hitler*, chapter 27, section 5.

77. Toland, *Adolf Hitler*, chapter 27, section 3.

78. Toland, *Adolf Hitler*, chapter 27, section 3.

79. Toland, *Adolf Hitler*, chapter 25, section 8.

80. Toland, *Adolf Hitler*, chapter 26, section 1.

81. Toland, *Adolf Hitler*, chapter 27.

82. Toland, *Adolf Hitler*, chapter 28, section 4.

83. Richard Evans, *The Third Reich at War: 1939–1945* (New York: Penguin Press, 2009). Kindle edition, part 6.

84. Toland, *Adolf Hitler*, chapter 29, section 3.

85. Samuel W. Mitcham, Jr., *Retreat to the Reich: The German Defeat in France, 1944* (Mechanicsburg, Pennsylvania: Stackpole, 2007), 57.

86. Original handwritten letter including Eisenhower's words, shapell.org/manuscript /General%20Eisenhower%20Ohrdruf%20Concentration%20Camp.

87. Shirer, *Berlin Diary*, 1104.

ABOUT THE AUTHOR

James Buckley Jr. is the author of more than 150 books for young readers on a dizzying variety of topics. He has written biographies for readers young and old on subjects including the Wright brothers, Roberto Clemente, Muhammad Ali, Milton Hershey, Betsy Ross, and Ernest Shackleton. His recent nonbiography work includes the *Animal Planet Animal Atlas*, *Bugopedia*, *Home Address: ISS*, and *Listopia: Planet Earth* (among other animal- or science-related books). He came to the world of books after a career in magazine publishing that included time at *Sports Illustrated* and NFL Publishing. Along with being a writer, he is the president of the Shoreline Publishing Group, a busy book producer based in Santa Barbara, California, where he lives with his wife, two children, loud dog, and two annoying cats.